# Your First Resume, Fifth Edition

## For Students and Anyone Preparing to Enter Today's Job Market

By
## Ron Fry

## THE CAREER PRESS INC.
Franklin Lakes, NJ

**YOUR FIRST RESUME, FIFTH EDITION**
Cover design by Johnson Design
Edited and Typeset by Nicole DeFelice
Printed in the U.S.A. by Book-mart Press

To order this title, please call toll-free 1-800-CAREER-1 (NJ and Canada: 201-848-0310) to order using VISA or MasterCard, or for further information on books from Career Press.

CAREER
PRESS

The Career Press, Inc., 3 Tice Road, PO Box 687
Franklin Lakes, NJ 07417
**www.careerpress.com**

**Library of Congress Cataloging-in-Publication Data**

Fry, Ronald
   Your first resume : for students and anyone preparing to enter today's job market / by
Ron Fry.— 5th ed.
      p. cm.
   Includes index.
   ISBN 1-56414-583-2 (paper)
   1. Résumés (Employment) 2.Job hunting. 3. High school students—Employment. 4.
College students—Employment.  I. Title.

HF5383 .F89 2001
650.14—dc21                                                                2001035875

# Contents

# You've Got 20 Seconds

Not long ago, my publishing company needed an editorial assistant—no experience necessary. Not surprisingly, a series of ads drew more than 375 responses. Since we're small and chronically short-staffed (hence, the hire!), we had to quickly and efficiently cull from this overabundance of proto-Hemingways a short list of five or six real possibilities.

Since we publish so many career books, we are probably more attuned than most firms to the vagaries and sorrows of the job search. We bear a special place in our hearts for those of you out there on the job trail. So, hearts on our collective sleeves, we found the time to pour over *every* word of *every* resume, no matter how sloppy, even the ones without cover letters.

No, we didn't. We did what every employer out there is going to do with *your* resume. We gave each resume barely 20 seconds to tell us what to do with it next—read it or toss it.

Twenty seconds. That's less time than a television commercial or a football huddle. But it really is all the time you've got to convince a screener in the human resources department or a busy hiring manager that your resume deserves a longer look.

The burgeoning of online job sites and resume postings doesn't change this time equation, except to make it *worse* for you. Many companies employ "key word" software to quickly scan the thousands of resumes they receive. Your resume may be rejected without even being seen by a real human being!

What is it that sends one resume to the "make" pile and another to the "break" can? As a seasoned job search author, I can definitively and categorically state, "That depends."

The ones that we tossed suffered from a variety of woes. One resume was a seventh-generation photocopy that was so fuzzy at the edges we worried that the candidate might be a little fuzzy, too. We found numerous typos in the cover letters, even four that managed to misspell "Career Press." And more than one was addressed to that cousin I don't have who insists on adding a redundant "e" to my name. A surprising number of others prominently featured an "Objective" that had nothing to do with the job we had open. The rest just didn't do anything to grab our attention or shout, "Me! Me! Read Me!"

The resumes of the five candidates we *did* choose to interview had some important things in common:

- Their resumes were neat, typeset, professionally printed on good stock, and formatted clearly and attractively.
- They were succinct—not necessarily short; they all utilized language that was clear, concise, and precise.
- They made us feel confident that we would not be wasting our too-precious time finding out more about these fabulous five.
- They clearly demonstrated that each applicant had the right education, qualifications, skills, and experience, plus a clear sense of purpose and pride.

Your challenge as a job seeker is to make a good first impression on the people doing the hiring—whether you "meet" them on paper or online. And the best way to do that is to write a winning resume.

*Your First Resume* exists to make sure *your* resume is one of the winners, the single piece of paper that cries out, even demands, an interview. Let all the others participate in the Trash Can Derby.

More than 250,000 copies of *Your First Resume* have been sold since 1988, so I must be doing something right. Yet, here I am, furiously revising and reformatting yet another new edition. Why?

While much of the advice I've given over the years is still valid, the job market is never static. Depending on the type of job you're seeking and the industry in which you're searching, you may be dealing with a market that favors you (the seller) or the employer (the buyer)—one that means a tough search against a sea of qualified candidates (the latter), or the chance to pick and choose from a plethora of potential opportunities (the former). Tomorrow, of course, you could find yourself in the opposite situation!

Whether jobs are scarce or plentiful, your resume must deliver in form and function. Your goal is to convince the employer to spend more time with you. To do that, you need a resume that looks good and clearly expresses what you have to offer. This brand-new fifth edition of *Your First Resume* will give you the ammunition to fight whatever battles you face.

Like previous editions, it also incorporates the direct-from-the-field feedback I continue to receive from your predecessors, along with a few changes I decided to make on my own. What's more, it aims to overcome the anxiety you may have about the uncertain job market with solid advice for selling yourself even to employers who can afford to be very choosy.

I think you'll find it more readable, usable, and helpful than ever before. But, of course, I always welcome your comments and good ideas. After all, this roller-coaster market guarantees that the sixth edition can't be far off.

Thank you in advance for all your help.

Ron Fry

June, 2001

# The Importance of Your First Resume

Fate saves most of us from what would be one of the most humbling experiences we could ever have—watching a recruiter or hiring manager examine our resumes. ("Examine" may be too generous a word; "barely glance at" is probably more accurate.) The experience would bring a whole new meaning to the word "dismissed."

Here you've taken the pains to deconstruct the story of your life onto a single sheet of paper, and some fathead is going to toss it, file it, or bury it in one of the many messy stacks on his desk...in 20 seconds or less.

Your resume is your calling card, and it had better get that manager's attention...*fast*. It must catch his eye, strike a nerve and get the right chemistry going—almost at a glance. Does this seem unreasonable, unfair, unintelligent, and arbitrary? Well, it is. It's also a reality you have to live with.

## "Hey, wait a minute! That's my life!"

That's what you'd scream if you could witness this humiliating spectacle. But you won't even be in the room. That's why I'm going to teach you how to develop a resume that does the screaming for you.

Your resume has a tough job: It has to grab that recruiter's attention as she gropes for that first cup of coffee. It has to convince her that you are one of the applicants that deserves a closer look.

Your resume is the proverbial foot in the door. Done correctly, it can give you the opportunity to move beyond *Your First Resume* to *Your First Interview* (which just so happens to be the subject of another one of my newly revised books).

As you prepare to write your resume, the first step is to relax. Putting together a resume can be a pleasant and rewarding experience...really! If you pay close attention to the steps outlined in this book and prepare your resume accordingly, you'll be on your way, happily blazing a successful career path. It's a trip worth taking, and *Your First Resume* will help you trod it in style. Let me give you an idea of what you'll find in this book—the who, what, why, when, and how of resumes.

## What is a resume?

A resume is a written document that attempts to communicate what you can offer an employer—by informing him about what you have *already* done—and motivate him to meet you. However, content alone cannot do that job. Presentation is almost equally important.

Perhaps I can give you a better fix on a definition by telling you what a resume is *not*. Having reviewed thousands of them in my roles as employer and counselor, I can tell you categorically that good resumes are not informal, lengthy, unfocused, lacking in pertinent detail, glib, highly personal, chatty, or overblown.

They *are*, on the other hand, characterized by the same qualities that are the hallmarks of any good advertisement.

First, the best resumes are *targeted*. They state a concise objective that positions the applicant on the road to a specific career.

For example, one resume that recently crossed my desk presented the applicant's career objective as follows: "Book sales position using enlightened marketing techniques to generate above-quota sales results." This well-thought-through objective gave me a clear picture of the benefits this applicant promised to bring to the job. It also communicated the fact that the applicant understood the reasons sales jobs existed in the publishing field in the first place. No surprise, she got the job.

Second, the resume supports this promise of performance. It provides the reasons that the applicant is best suited for the job.

And finally, it does all of this *honestly*. That means you must be honest with yourself in developing a career goal for which you are truly suited. Then, you must make sure that the resume and you, the "merchandise" it supposedly describes, are not cut from completely different cloth.

Wallflowers should not present themselves as killer salespeople, and those best suited for actuarial work probably should not describe themselves as stand-up comedians. Eventually, the truth will come out—probably during the interview—and assure you of only one thing—failure.

Remember: Along with your cover letter, your resume is your initial "first-person" introduction to a prospective employer. It *must* be a professional-looking document that clearly communicates all of your qualifications. It also *must* be absolutely error-free—no typos, no misplaced commas, no misspellings.

## Who needs a resume?

Everyone. If you are about to finish high school or college, receive a vocational education certificate, make the transition from a military career to civilian life, or reenter the work force after any substantial interruption, get ready to write a resume!

As someone "new" to the game—about to enter or reenter the work force on any level—you are making the transition from one mode of life to another. Your resume is the vehicle that will enable you to get there.

Even if you're just applying for a summer job, internship, or part-time, after-school work, you should have a resume, even if employers don't always require or even ask for one when filling temporary positions. A well-designed, well-prepared resume will set you apart from all those others who *didn't* take the time to summarize their education, skills, and qualifications. Your resume will present you exactly the way you *want* to be perceived—professional, competent, ready to work!

## When should I prepare my resume?

Give yourself as much time as possible. If you're a student, I recommend that you prepare a draft of your first resume just as you enter your senior year in high school or college, refine it at the mid-year break, and finalize it no later than February 1st. This will give you ample time to plan, execute, edit, refine, and proofread it. If you're no longer in school, start working on your resume three to six months before you plan to begin your job search.

However, you shouldn't plan your resume until your objectives have crystallized and you have some knowledge of the fundamentals of the job search process. Remember: You're not seeking a baby-sitting assignment or paper delivery route. You're after a *real* job, and you need to know where you're going in order to map out how to get there.

## What you'll learn in this book

Chapter 1 will show you how to decide where you are going. It will lead you through the steps for completing your own "Where Do I Fit?" chart (with samples you can use as a guide). If you've been taking ballet lessons since the age of five, are musical, athletic, and the best tap dancer in class, possess lots of energy, and perhaps a touch of tunnel vision, you're probably already well on your way to a career in the chorus line.

For most of you, the choice is not so clear-cut and obvious. You can, however, narrow the scope of this decision-making process by focusing on the career areas in which your skills (and the other things you'll learn about yourself in Chapter 1) indicate you will most likely succeed.

Chapter 2 will show you how to narrow down the career areas most appropriate for you. One surefire tip is to study the trade publications that cover the industry in which you're interested. You'll get an overview of the industry, a flavor of what it's like, and a taste of how it sees itself. This will also give you a first-hand look at the people involved in the industry, which might make you even more motivated...or lead to a quick change of plans!

## Challenging Catch-22

You can't get a job without experience, and you can't get experience without a job. Well, there are a number of ways to get around *that* conundrum long before you have to start pounding the pavement. In Chapter 3, I'll introduce you to a variety of ways you can build credentials—and even get some real on-the-job experience—before you start interviewing.

## Finding the right fit

Birds of a feather *do* flock together. And different companies tend to attract particular "species" of employees. The personality of the birds that predominate is the company's corporate culture. Is it a "loose" atmosphere with jean-clad creatives running amok? Or a buttoned-down, blue-suited autocracy with timed coffee breaks?

The more you know about the companies you're considering, the better off you'll be. For those of you—and that should be *all* of you—who want to research a specific company and/or job description, Chapter 4 will give you the necessary hints and resources.

## Becoming resourceful

You don't have to be a private detective to locate various agencies, programs, and Web sites that can serve as a link to job leads in your community. There are a whole host of resources out there, many of them free. Chapter 5 lists the places to go for help, including a variety of up-to-date online job sites.

## You say you heard it through the grapevine?

An informational interview (don't panic!) can bring you face-to-face with someone who's already got the job you want. But instead of sweating through a for-real interview, *you* will be asking most of the questions: "What is it like to work in this industry?" "What do you like best—and least—about your job?" "What kinds of things should I be sure to include on my resume?"

You might want to go online and chat with somebody in your chosen field. The Internet has its own yellow pages bursting with addresses for every interest, and there are thousands of chat rooms in which to meet people and trade information about career plans.

It's hard for many people to believe that "word of mouth" is the loudest trumpet proclaiming what and where the jobs are. But it is. By talking to friends (old and new), acquaintances, and relatives (and *their* friends, acquaintances, and relatives) about your career plans, you'll soon build an ever-growing network of contacts. Once all of these people know a little bit about you and what you're looking for, they can refer you to prospective employers. Of course, they may expect you to return the favor somewhere along the line. That's how networking works! Chapter 6 will show you how to implement this very important process and begin to develop your own lifelong network.

## Getting the grades

Believe it or not, there's still some work to do before you start writing your resume! Collecting all your records—high school report cards, college transcripts, detailed employment data, lists of activities and clubs, etc.—is the one thing left to do. Chapter 7 will help you organize all of these records and provides a number of forms to help you summarize the information.

## If it looks like a resume, then it must be a resume

It's time to write. But before you can commit words to paper, you have to choose a format for your resume. In Chapter 8, I discuss the various organizational formats that you can use (chronological, functional, combination), the information to include or omit, and some basic rules to follow in preparing any resume, no matter how simple or complex. I'll also cover the electronic variety, as well as some advice on how to post your resume online.

In Chapter 9, I'll help you edit, rewrite, proofread, and polish your gem until all of your strengths, qualifications, and accomplishments shine through.

## Sample these

You'll have the opportunity to review real resumes that real people have used to secure job interviews in Chapter 10. Multiple examples of those using the three basic formats are included, plus examples for special situations, such as military personnel returning to the civilian work force. Whether you aspire to be an administrative assistant, a financial analyst, or (eventually) CEO, you'll find a sample that will help you devise your own selling resume.

## Letter perfect

There are two different types of letters you should be prepared to write as you progress through your job search. A cover letter will accompany your resume in reply to an ad or cold call or it will serve as an inquiry. After a job interview, you'll send off a follow-up letter. Both letters are covered in Chapter 11, along with several samples of each type.

## No more sweaty palms

Finally, your hours of preparation have paid off—you're sitting opposite the operations supervisor of the ABC Widget Company. It's your first job interview! An entry-level sales slot is open, and you're being considered. Nervous? Who wouldn't be? Follow the tips in Chapter 12, and you'll learn how to turn the interviewing process to your advantage. By knowing the types of questions you can expect, you can practice your answers—as well as the types of questions you'll volley back.

You'll also find hints on dress, demeanor, posture, body language, the proper way to fill out a job application, and how to handle psychological tests, which many large companies now utilize.

## For women (mainly)

Yes, women have come a long way, but they still face pressures in the job search process most men don't. What's more, women and other minority groups are much more likely to encounter subtle discrimination or unfair interview questions. Today's working mothers may also have to answer for taking time off to raise a family. Chapter 13 touches on all of these issues.

## The start of something big

Exhilerating, challenging, rewarding—that's how I've described the process of constructing your first resume. This introduction is only a taste of what's to come. Take the time to read through the book and complete the necessary exercises, lists, and charts—it will give you the self-confidence you need to successfully maneuver through the entry-level job search minefield.

Waiting at the conclusion is the sense of accomplishment you'll feel when you get the job that's absolutely perfect for *you*.

# Chapter 1

# Who Are You—*Really?*

This chapter, the most basic of all, may well be the most important. Why? Because it will help you construct the foundation upon which you'll erect the structure of your entire job search.

And all to answer one simple question: Who are you? Just because you're reading a career book, don't *only* think of what you've accomplished in school or work, or how you might describe yourself to a prospective employer. Who are you as a *person?*

Your unique skills, likes, dislikes, strengths, weaknesses, and hidden abilities should all factor into any career decisions you make. Identifying, listing, analyzing, and interpreting them is a process that will pay significant dividends.

When you're through with the series of exercises in this chapter, you will have some concept (perhaps for the first time) of the person lurking behind that face in the mirror. More importantly for the purposes of this book, you'll also have a much better idea of where *you* fit into the broad puzzle called the job market.

## Your career commitment

In the course of an average working lifetime, you'll spend up to 60,000 hours exercising a given set of skills. Living a work life that is productive and fulfilled depends to a large extent on how well you identify and utilize your dominant skills and talents, especially right from the beginning. If you correctly match your skills and interests to the right industry, company, and job functions, chances are, your work life will be a successful and happy one. Should you be off the mark in the self-evaluation process, you may wind up in the wrong industry, at the wrong company, and/or at the wrong job.

The results will be what you would expect from any mismatch—sub-par performance and frustration. Nobody needs a mid-life crisis at 22!

## Nobody can be a "jack of all trades"

It is the rare individual who is superior, or even good, in every subject. (If you are, count your blessings and apply for Sainthood at the door, please.) Most of us are a little better in one or another. Some of us simply *like* one subject more than another—and don't think *that* doesn't change our attitude toward it.

For example, skill with numbers and spatial relations might come easily to you, but you may have no ear for music or languages. Or, you may find it remarkably easy to communicate in writing or art, but have not the faintest clue why Pythagoras came up with his Theorem...or why you should care. Some people can build the Taj Mahal out of toothpicks during their lunch hour. Others, like me, can't glue two boards together.

## Go with what you know

My advice is to be thankful for whatever native-born talents you possess and to sharpen and use those gifts. First, give some thought about the subjects you like and dislike, using the chart on page 15 to identify them. These lists will help you evaluate potential job openings and find those most suited to *your* skills and talents. Let's face it, if your research indicates a particular job will require heavy number-crunching and you despise math, it probably isn't the job for you!

## So, what are you selling?

Every one of you has innate skills that will tilt you toward the particular career path for which you are uniquely qualified. The trick is to identify and strengthen them. Some are obvious and quantifiable: typing speed, a sense of numbers, an ear for music or languages, artistic ability. Others are less obvious, but equally important: the ability to listen, to store information, to relate well with people.

Your challenge now is to consider this mass of raw ingredients and decide which personality characteristics to present to prospective employers—and *how* to present them.

Think of your skills as falling into three major areas: people, information, and manual.

# Evaluation of subject areas

List the subject areas/courses you liked most:

_____

_____

_____

_____

_____

List the subject areas/courses you liked least:

_____

_____

_____

_____

_____

List the courses in which you got the best grades:

_____

_____

_____

_____

_____

List the courses in which you got the worst grades:

_____

_____

_____

_____

_____

# Are you a "people person"?

This category includes those skills and abilities that enable you to interact comfortably and effectively with other people. Do people tend to trust you? Do you like to work in teams? Do you love to speak in public? Are you attuned to the moods and body language of your friends and co-workers?

# Or would you prefer things in black and white?

Computer printouts, accounting ledgers, inventory statistics—look at the desks of information-oriented people and you'll probably find plenty of data. Informational skills are manifested in an ability to analyze, observe, evaluate, and rearrange statistics and facts to give them a life of their own. Raw data becomes sales forecasts, quality control reports, and profit and loss statements.

# Maybe you're a hands-on kind of guy or gal

We all know people who are "good with their hands," whose manual and/or physical dexterity seemingly enable them to build or fix anything. If you can assemble your kid brother's bike in 42 seconds or build a tree house that belongs in *Architectural Digest*, you may belong in this group.

# Time to make a choice

Now that you understand how to group the various ingredients of your personality, it's time to sift each one of them through a set of screens to assess how you'll fit in various employment situations. This is the "Where Do I Fit?" part of the process.

Chances are, you'll find yourself favoring one of the three basic skill areas described on pages 17 to 19. But it's not necessary to limit yourself. If you find you have sufficient skills in more than one broad category, then work through the "Where Do I Fit?" exercise as many times as necessary.

On the following pages, I've set up three simple tables—one for each of the three primary skill categories. In each chart, I've cataloged basic skills by type, linked them to a work- or job-related characteristic, as well as a sampling (though by no means all-inclusive) of career areas. Use the three fill-in-the-blanks worksheets on pages 20, 21, and 22 to record information about each of your personal strengths.

This is an exercise to demonstrate how you can translate a specific skill into a work characteristic and, eventually, a specific job description/ career. It is *not* in any way meant to be an all-inclusive, confining method that pigeonholes you into one job or another. So please don't consider it the end of the process, just a step along the way.

## WHERE DO I FIT CHART: PEOPLE SKILLS

| Skill | Work characteristic | Career |
|---|---|---|
| Taking instruction | Pay attention, carry out orders | Administrative |
| Serving | Execute wishes of others | Public relations, nursing |
| Sensing, feeling | "Read" others' feelings | Telemarketing, sales |
| ✓ Communicating | Give and take information | Creative writing |
| Persuading | Generate action in others | Advertising |
| Performing, amusing | Work before a group | Law, acting |
| ✓ Managing | Behave in a way that achieves an objective | Public affairs, strategic planning |
| Negotiating | Give and take to achieve compromise | Politics, sales, psychiatry, social work |
| ✓ Leading | Motivate by example | Executive |
| Treating | Improve a condition | Counseling, medicine |
| Advising | Give expert advice | Research |
| ✓ Training | Impart new information, ideas, procedures | Teaching, drama coaching |

# WHERE DO I FIT CHART: INFORMATION SKILLS

| Skill | Work characteristic | Career |
|---|---|---|
| Observing | Good student of behavior | Accounting, analysis |
| Comparing | Identify similarities, dissimilarities | Quality control inspecting |
| Copying, storing | Good memory skills | Translating |
| Computing | Mathematical dexterity | Banking, finance, computer programming |
| Researching | Persistence | Science, chemistry, engineering |
| Analyzing | Seeing the whole and its parts | Movie/book criticism |
| Organizing | Adept at structure | Administration |
| Evaluating | Good judgment | Vocational guidance |
| Visualizing | Symbolic perception | Interior design, architecture |
| Improving, adapting | Updating | Editing, journalism |
| Creating | Turning data into something new | Securities analysis |
| Designing | Molding, reshaping | Package coordinating |
| Planning | Priority and sequencing skills | Systems engineering |
| Expediting | Speed | Office managing |
| Achieving | Reach or surpass goals | Athletic coaching |

## WHERE DO I FIT CHART: MANUAL SKILLS

| Skill | Work characteristic | Career |
|---|---|---|
| Handling | Use of hands/body | Contruction worker |
| Physical strength | Athletic coordination | Machine operation, metal work |
| Earth and nature | Making nature work for you | Landscaping |
| Feeding | Machine-literate | Assembly-line work |
| Monitoring | Service machinery | Mechanics |
| Mechanical | Manual dexterity | Carpentry, painting, bookbinding |
| Vehicle skills | Regulating, controlling | Airplane Pilot |
| Precision | Work within set limits | Surgery, diamond cutting |
| Assembling | Organizing | Plumbing, electric |
| Repairing | Understand how things operate | TV repair |

## WHERE DO I FIT CHART: PEOPLE SKILLS

**Skill**          **Work characteristic**      **Career**

## WHERE DO I FIT CHART: INFORMATION SKILLS

| Skill | Work characteristic | Career |
| --- | --- | --- |

## WHERE DO I FIT CHART: MANUAL SKILLS
**Skill**              **Work characteristic**      **Career**

# What turns you on?

Before we are finished, we must complete one more step. It's also important to identify the primary motivator that affects your performance, the one which determines the skill sets to which you are most drawn. In other words, what turns you on?

What's interesting about this exercise is, although there are a vast number of skills, the reasons for your choosing one career over another may be reduced to one of only five factors: celebrity, money, power, affiliation, and fulfillment. Discovering which of these is your primary motivator will help you make the right career choice.

## *Life is a stage*

Do you want to be a star? If so, you must choose a career path that will give you the chance to achieve the *fame* you desire. But don't think only "artsy" careers, like actor, rock star, or anchor for the "Sunday News" can put you in the limelight. An activist corporate leader eager to cultivate an image as a mover and shaker might be driven by the same lust for celebrity. The engineer who yearns to become the commercial spokesperson for a new line of automobiles has more than car sales on his mind!

## *Money talks*

If your personal creed can be summarized as "I want, therefore I am," *wealth* is clearly your primary motivator. So be prepared to abandon hobbies that won't translate into the Big Bucks and look to investment banking, Wall Street, or your own business in your search for the golden goddess. (An MBA from Stanford wouldn't hurt.) Since the big payoffs are usually found in short-term, high-risk/high-reward undertakings, any desire for safety or security should be jettisoned. Make sure you are quick, flexible, risk-oriented, self-centered, and more confident in your abilities than Anna Nicole Smith on a date with an octogenarian.

## *I can buy and sell you*

*Power* is a difficult motivator to admit to because it comes with so much negative baggage. After all, power corrupts, right? The flip side, of course, is the power of the printed word or the power of government to correct social ills. If you must push the power button, choose an area in which you will quickly be able to assume power and exercise it. An office manager in charge of a large clerical staff has real power. So do many journalists. Choose a career that gives you control over people, issues, and/or attitudes.

## *Good work!*

If you believe virtue is its own reward, *fulfillment* is a prime motivator in your choice of careers. Go for a job that allows you to do more for others than for yourself. Work for a charity, become a legal-aid lawyer, join a religious order.

*Part of the team*

To people motivated by *affiliation*, finding or creating the right work environment is much more important than money, power, or fame. (It's their way of being fulfilled.) If you fall into this category, know what your potential employer stands for and be sure you're comfortable with it.

It will be important for you to work with people you like, those who share a similar outlook on life and work. If strict rules make you uncomfortable, consider pursuing a career on the creative side of advertising, where jeans and sneakers and a modicum of craziness are *de rigueur*. If you enjoy wearing dark suits and white shirts—and being surrounded by similarly attired co-workers in a stricter corporate environment—call your nearest Fortune 100 corporation.

# The value of a second opinion

Would you get a second opinion before undergoing major surgery? Of course you would. So, why go through the practice of choosing your life's work all by yourself? If you think of yourself as outgoing and charismatic, does that mean that you really are? If you think you are the most creative kid on campus, would your classmates all readily agree? Let's face it, all of us practice the fine art of fooling ourselves from time to time.

So after you've completed the various exercises in this chapter, review them with a friend, relative or parent. These second opinions may reveal some aspects of your self-description on which you and the rest of the world differ. If so, discuss them, learn from them and, if necessary, change some of your conclusions.

# Applying what you've learned

You've answered a series of very important questions: What can I do? What do I like to do? What drives me? How do others see me? What are my values? You have begun to get some insight into the product you're preparing to market—yourself. It's not a bad picture, is it?

At this juncture, adopt a seller's attitude. That is, choose the exact career path you want to pursue, rather than seeing "what's out there" and applying haphazardly for anything and everything. For some of you, the direction will be obvious—you and a career will seem made for each other.

Others will need to set their targets—define those career areas that seem to promise the greatest likelihood of success.

Once you have decided on your list, you're ready to enter the research portion of the job search process. Chapter 2 spells out how you can target and identify those industries in which your skills will be needed and learn all about them.

# Researching Your Career Path

Searching for a job is mainly a process of elimination: You must consider and research as many options as possible, then narrow down your choices.

This chapter will help you begin this elimination process by demonstrating how to assess the current state and potential for growth of the industries or professions you might wish to consider.

Even if you think you know exactly what you want to do, researching your preferred industry or profession will, at the very least, affirm your choice. Additionally, such general research will point out negative factors you must consider before making your final choice.

Doing your own homework also will ensure that you don't behave like all too many job seekers. They check the classified ads, call a few executive recruiters and, basically, wait for things to happen to them.

The fact is that the overwhelming majority of jobs—some experts say 85 percent—are not advertised in the classified section nor turned over to outside recruiters.

As a result, it is up to you to go out and find yourself a job. (That's why they call it a job *search*!)

## Separating the winners from the losers

This process will help you develop a broad understanding of the winners and losers on the economic scene and why some industries and professions offer better long-term opportunities than others.

For a very broad overview of any industry, consult the U.S. Bureau of Labor Statistics (*stats.bls.gov*), which uses business and economic trends and changing demographics to chart expected growth in employment for occupations in every industry over a 10-year period. The most current set of projections (issued in November 1999) covers the 1998-2008 period. Online quarterly updates of the *Occupational Outlook Handbook* are available at the same site, along with a wealth of industry and overall economic information. The most current [2000-2001] edition of *The Career Guide to Industries*, companion to the *OOH*, discusses 42 industries.

## The only thing you can depend on is change

The fundamental profile of the U.S. economy has been changing since the 1970s—its historical emphasis on "making things" is waning, as manufacturing becomes more efficient and inexpensive overseas.

However, this massive restructuring did not result in tremendous unemployment because jobs were being created in industries that were marketing- or sales-driven, those that concentrated on finance, promotion, or the dissemination of information, and those that provided services.

Nevertheless, many old-line industries, such as Big Steel, are expected to continue their decline. Further complicating this picture is the "shake-out" in service and information industries. Unprecedented layoffs among white-collar workers in both service and manufacturing sectors of the economy began in the early 1990s. Though we are currently at "full" employment, I can't think of a high-tech company out there that hasn't announced layoffs in the first quarter of 2001. Many entry-level jobs have been made obsolete by ever more powerful computers and networks (even as the companies that make them announce new layoffs!).

As the new century dawned, dotcom mania came and went, seemingly in a heartbeat. One moment, every Stanford MBA was starting a new company in his or her dorm room and counting the millions in venture capital raised. Yet, just a week ago, an article described the most recent recruiting fair for Stanford MBAs as "desolate; a full 25 percent of the companies scheduled to attend didn't even show up."

The economic downturn in 2000 and the first quarter of 2001 forced many corporations to slash spending on infrastructure, equipment, even research. Entire industries were nearly decimated as Wall Street flushed shares of even the biggest names in high tech down the proverbial toilet. So, while some entry-level candidates are finding little or no change in the job market, or are even in the enviable position of choosing between competing bonuses, others are finding recruiting visits cancelled or even previous job offers rescinded. It is a decidedly mixed bag!

So, where are you, the new job hunter, supposed to look?

## Hot prospects

While demand for many jobs is cooling, some areas are just heating up. You just have to know where to look. For instance, even a quick look at recent census data will reveal that a career in health care, especially in areas catering to the elderly, is far more promising than one designing children's clothing. Why? Because America is graying. By the year 2030, senior citizens will represent 25 percent of the population—nearly double the current figure. Those industries targeted to provide for the elderly will certainly benefit.

Although there is a mini-version of the Baby Boom going on now, prospects for once-flourishing industries focused on children's products are not what they once were. However, childcare has become a priority for an increasing number of two-income families. And there are simply not enough teachers to go around...anywhere.

See how it works?

## Buying time

Even though it is fashionable to revile the 1980s as the decade of consumption, our society is still an indulgent one. The interest in time-consuming leisure activities—travel, exercise, family—has not yet peaked. But then, neither have the demands that employers are placing on our time.

As a result, a significant portion of our service-oriented economy is now dedicated to supplying an increasingly valuable commodity—time. Consider, for instance, the explosive growth of the fast-food business. Other service industries pegged to affording people more freedom in their time off from work will probably continue to grow in the years ahead.

## Pick a winner

Each year, the wise men who report and comment on the world of business publish their lists of growth industries. These are areas that, based on a number of economic and marketing indicators, appear to offer the best potential. In addition to health care, the environment and global trade seem to be on everyone's current list. Why not practice a little crystal-ball analysis of your own? It's simple. Just focus on the demand side of the supply-demand equation. If your common sense tells you the products of a particular industry will surely be in demand, you've identified a growth industry. If it is one that interests you, all the better.

## Get the inside line

Now that you know about targeting industry winners and losers, it's time to put your expertise to work. Let's assume for a moment that you want to investigate the restaurant/food service business.

The first thing to do is become acquainted with a key reference resource—the various volumes of the Standard Rate and Data Service (SRDS), all of which are available in most libraries. The volume in which you're interested is Business Publications. In it you'll find a list, by industry, of the thousands of business (or trade) magazines currently being published. For example, under "Restaurant/Food Service," you'll find the following listings: *Bill of Fare, Catering Today, Chef Institutional, Cooking for Profit, Food Management, Institutional Distribution, Restaurant News, Restaurant Business, Restaurant Hospitality,* and *Restaurants & Institutions.*

You'll find similar listings for all the other industries and professions you've targeted.

These publications are prime sources of information. Start reading them regularly (many are collected in metropolitan public libraries). Write for recent issues of the leading publications for the fields you've targeted. If you make reading a weekly practice, you will accomplish a number of important goals. You'll begin to absorb information about:

- The industry as a whole.
- Major companies in the field.
- Trends, new products, and the general outlook for specific product categories.
- Major players in the industry—both companies and individuals.
- Industry/professional jargon or "buzzwords."

In addition, published interviews with leading practitioners in the field will give you insight on how they approach their specific jobs.

Hint: Look for news about recent or forthcoming mergers and acquisitions. Such movement often leads to shifts in personnel needs—while some highly compensated pros may hit the streets as duplicated positions are eliminated, lower-paid, entry-level people may be waltzing in the front door.

## The bottom line

You can get a good indication of the strength of an industry by looking at the financial results of any of its leading companies. All publicly held corporations are required by law to issue annual reports, which include this detailed financial data.

You can call a company's headquarters and ask to receive a free copy. However, many metropolitan libraries maintain collections of annual reports from major corporations and most are now available online.

## A very special reading list

Here's a primary list of research sources, most of which should be available in any good reference library. These references are essential to garner more specific information about companies you've targeted:

- The *Encyclopedia of Business Information Sources* lists some 25,000 sources on more than a thousand specific subjects, including directories, associations, and more. The biannual *Directories in Print* organizes companies by industry. The annual *Job Seekers Guide to Public and Private Companies* covers 25,000 companies, with detailed information on specific job titles and openings for each. (All from Gale Research Inc.)
- Directory of Corporate Affiliations and Directory of Leading Private Companies (Reed Reference Publishing, New Providence, NJ 07974)

- Dun and Bradstreet's family of corporate reference resources: the *Million Dollar Directory* (160,000 companies with a net worth of more than $500,000), *Top 50,000 Companies* (those with a mini-mum net worth of just under $2 million), and *Business Rankings* (details on the nation's top 7,500 firms). Another volume—*Reference Book of Corporate Managements/ America's Corporate Leaders* —provides detailed biographical data on the principal officers and directors of some 12,000 corporations. (Who says you can't find out about the quirks and hobbies of your interviewer?) All of these volumes are available in most libraries or from Dun's Marketing Services (3 Sylvan Way, Parsippany, NJ 07054).

- *Moody's Industry Review* (available from Moody's Investors Service, Inc., 99 Church St., New York, NY 10007).

- *Standard and Poors' Register of Corporations, Directors and Executives* includes corporate listings for more than 45,000 firms and 72,000 biographical listings (available from Standard and Poors, 25 Broadway, New York, NY 10004).

- *Thomas's Register of American Manufacturers* (Thomas Publishing Company, 1 Penn Plaza, New York, NY 10110). Annual profile of more than 150,000 manufacturers. Features information on primary products and services plus more than 100,000 trade and brand names.

- *Ward's Business Directory*, a four-volume reference work that includes listings of nearly 100,000 companies, the majority of them privately held, and details that are usually most difficult to acquire about such firms such as number of employees, annual sales, etc. (Gale Research Inc.)

- The *Standard Directory of Advertisers* (also known as the Advertiser Red Book, because of its bright red cover) lists more than 17,000 companies that commit some portion of their budgets to advertising and promotion. It is available in two editions—classified and geographical. Major product lines and the agencies to whom they are assigned are listed, as well as names and job functions of key marketing personnel at the listed companies and their agencies. (121 Chanlon Rd. New Providence, NJ 07974 or *www.redbooks.com*)

- *The Fortune 500* is an annual compilation by *Fortune* magazine of the top U.S. businesses, ranked by sales. It will become particularly important later in your search, when you're targeting specific companies. At that time, it will enable you to analyze not only where a particular company ranks in the overall U.S. economy, but also whether it is falling or on the rise, and how it measures up against other companies in its field. (Time, Inc. 1271 Avenue of the Americas NY, NY 10020)

Some other potential sources of leads include *The Oxbridge Directory of Newsletters* (check your library), a listing of thousands of newsletters in a plethora of industries that might give you some ideas and names. *The Professional Exhibits Directory* (Gale Research Inc.) lists more than 2,000 trade shows and conventions. Why not consider attending some to learn more about the companies and products out there?

Finally, here are some primary sources that you should turn to now and then to complete your research: *The Wall Street Journal, Barron's, Business Week, Fortune, Forbes, Industry Week, Nation's Business, National Business Employment Weekly, and Inc.* Naturally, the trade magazines that you've been studying (and to which you've already subscribed, I hope!) offer a steady stream of very specific information. Become as familiar as possible with the companies' jargon, as topics covered indicate how the industry is evolving.

## Success by association

Trade associations are generally nonprofit organizations set up to advance the fortunes and concerns of a particular industry or profession. The membership of the American Association of Advertising Agencies (4As), for example, is comprised of about 700 advertising agencies (including virtually all of the big guns). The association's aim is to improve the image of and professionalism within the advertising profession.

Many trade associations are excellent sources for industry data and statistics as well as general employment trends and specific opportunities. Four good resources are the *Encyclopedia of Associations* and *Business Organizations, Agencies and Publications Directory* (both from Gale Research Inc.), *National Trade and Professional Associations of the United States* (Columbia Books, Inc.) and the *Association Yellow Book* (Monitor Publishing Co.). If you want to work for an association that serves a particular industry or profession, these same references will give you the information you need.

Other terrific resources are job fairs—informal get-togethers at which company recruiters and prospective employees can interact in a trade show-style atmosphere. The business section of your local paper will generally include announcements of those being held in your area. A more general resource is the *Career and Job Fair Finder* (College Placement Council, Inc.), which should be in your public or school library.

## "Ask the person who owns one"

Some years ago, this advice was used as the theme for a highly successful automobile advertising campaign. The prospective car buyer was encouraged to find out about the product by asking the (supposedly) most trustworthy judge of all—someone who was already an owner.

You can use the same approach in your job search. You have relatives or friends already out in the workplace. Contact these resources. You'll be amazed at how readily they'll answer your questions. At a minimum, you'll want to learn how the industry is doing, what its long-term prospects are, the kinds of personalities it favors, the rate of employee turnover, and the availability of training. (Chapter 5 will help you cast your net far and wide.)

## The other end of the iceberg

You are now better prepared to choose those industries and professions that meet your own list of criteria. There are, however, some major issues you'll want information about before pursuing a particular career:

**Promotion.** If you are aggressive about your career plans, look for industries that are growing and companies that traditionally promote from within.

**Training.** Look for industries and companies in which your early tenure will actually be a period of on-the-job training—hopefully companies dedicated to training over the long term.

**Salary.** Some industries are high-paying, some are not.

**Benefits.** Look for industries in which health insurance, vacation pay, retirement plans, stock purchase opportunities, and other important employee benefits are extensive...and company-paid.

## Keep on digging

Chapter 4 will give you a well-designed blueprint on how to research particular companies and specific career areas (job functions). But first, it's time to address the ubiquitous Catch 22 for first-time job seekers: How do you get experience when you need experience to get a job?

# Chapter 3

# Getting Real-World Experience Early

You know that old Catch-22: You have to have experience to get a good job—but how can you get experience if nobody will hire you?

There are a number of ways—both structured and innovative—to get the kind of practical experience that will impress prospective employers. The important thing to realize is that, if you lock yourself up in an ivory tower during your college years, waiting until you graduate to get experience, you may be locking yourself *out* of even entry-level access to many professions, such as science, law, and medicine.

These days, you can expect employers to look very closely at how you, as a prospective candidate, have *already* applied what you've learned in the classroom to real-world situations. Graduate students, especially, are expected to come into a first job ready to contribute right away. Most employers want evidence that new employees will not only fit in, but be ready to pitch in from day one.

According to the U.S. Bureau of Labor Statistics, at least 20 percent of all college graduates will finally settle for positions that don't require a college education. So, if you don't want to end up as a receptionist or selling shoes in the local department store, I suggest you read on.

Ideally, you will have already served one or more internships within your field of study during your college years. If you have, bravo. Many employers recruit directly from internship and co-op (work/study) programs because they've had many opportunities to see you in action. They have, in effect, taken you for a "test drive." I'll talk in greater detail about internships and related co-op experiences in just a moment.

But first, suppose you can't afford to take a low-paying—or no-paying—position just to get experience. You have tuition and living expenses to worry about! Don't worry. Your paying jobs have you operating out there in the real world. In Chapter 8, you'll find many examples of how to frame the experience you have gained working part-time and at summer jobs on your resume. In this chapter, however, I'll also give you some ideas for how to "manufacture" the kind of experience that will impress a prospective employer with your initiative and problem-solving abilities.

## Internships: not just for gofers

You may have it in your head that interning is just another form of slave labor. That you'll be locked away in a little room all day, filing, stapling, and collating until your hands are as callused as Scrooge's.

The stories of many of the interns profiled in a recently published directory of internship opportunities paint a different picture. There is the graduate student who read manuscripts and book proposals and made recommendations on their fitness for publication; the college junior, set on becoming an investment banker, who wrote competitive analysis reports for the company that later hired him; and the future marketing manager who coordinated college promotions for a hot new magazine.

I'll bet I've got your interest now! Let's take a closer look at what internships involve.

An internship is a goal-oriented, monitored work or service position that may last as little as a month or as long as two years. Internships can be part-time or full-time, paid or unpaid. To be eligible for most internships, you will have to meet minimum age and education requirements. While most interns are undergraduate and graduate students, you may be working side-by-side with senior citizens, mid-career executives, and international transplants.

The key element that distinguishes internships from most other short-term jobs is that they involve a "learning agenda." You and your supervisor will probably sit down and discuss what you want to learn from the experience before you start working. Some internships fit into a set educational program, so the work you do will be carefully monitored and evaluated for academic credit. Others give you more flexibility to balance your own learning objectives with the work that needs to be done by the company that hires you.

Whether you work in a bank or a wildlife refuge, you should, even in a short time, have many opportunities to:

- Gain practical experience in a new field.
- Learn about a company from the inside.
- Learn new skills, such as how to use computer software that is commonly used in the industry.
- Wander around the workplace and check out what kind of work other people are doing.
- Ask a million questions. People will be open and even feel obliged to share information with you—much more so than if you were trying to "break in" the hard way, as secretary or administrative assistant.

- ◆   Make contacts that can hire you or help you find another job.
- ◆   Try on a career without making a permanent commitment.

Some internships include additional benefits, over and above a salary (which, in many cases but certainly not all, is little more than minimum wage). As an intern, you may receive special training, housing, meals, medical benefits, and placement services.

If you're worried that there aren't enough internship positions to go around, don't be. Due to funding shortages, many government, arts, and nonprofit organizations could not operate without the involvement of interns, both during the summer and full-time. For a local listing of internships available in your field, stop by your college placement office.

If you graduate from college without a job, an internship can fill a hole in your resume—and introduce you to a prospective employer. In this case, your work experience might also become a multi-week "interview."

# The co-op connection

Although many people tend to use the terms "co-op" and "internship" interchangeably, there is a difference. Co-op (short for Cooperative Education) programs allow college students to integrate periods of paid training in business, industry, nonprofit, and government agencies with classroom study.

Unlike many internships, co-op positions are always paid. In addition, co-op assignments must last at least one semester, and you may be able to earn college credit for the work you do on your co-op assignment.

The names of large, well-known co-op sponsors such as Douglas Aircraft Co., Hewlett-Packard, J.C. Penney Co., and Pricewaterhouse Coopers can do wonders for your resume. But you may not need your resume after you graduate. Many companies, nonprofits, and agencies that sponsor co-op programs use them to recruit entry-level people.

Typically, co-op programs are open to undergraduates who are currently enrolled in school, have declared a major field of study, and have completed a minimum number of course units. Graduate students may also be eligible for some co-op positions. Students are typically placed with co-op employers through the college placement office. Some take a leave of absence from school to work full-time for one semester and then return to classes for the next, thereby *alternating* work experience with classroom study. On this plan, you may have to graduate a semester later than you'd originally planned, but the experience you gain should make the delay well worth it. Some students choose to work 20 or so hours a week while carrying a full academic course load, then work full-time during the summer.

How much can you make on a co-op assignment? Your hourly rate will depend on your employer, the nature of your assignment, and your academic major and level. Since co-op employees are considered temporary personnel, you won't be eligible for benefits.

Visit your college or university placement office to learn whether or not there is a co-op program for your school and, if there is, how to participate. Typically, the process of finding a "match" is very similar to the process of finding a job. You'll check current listings of co-op vacancies in the college placement office, request that your co-op application and resume be referred to specific employers, and undergo a pre-screening telephone interview and one or more on-site interviews over the course of several months. Some employers conduct interviews on campus. On average, it takes at least one semester to register, actively apply, and finally be placed in a co-op position.

## Placing a value on volunteer work

Getting involved in extracurricular activities (and I mean getting *involved*, not just attending one meeting, snatching some cookies, and leaving early) can really pay dividends when it comes to courting prospective employers.

In addition to the initiative you showed in joining, your involvement may demonstrate evidence of your ability to act as a leader, handle responsibility, and get along with many different kinds of people—all important work-related qualifications.

Many professional and community service organizations have chapters on campus and welcome (in many cases, they are *desperate* for) help in planning, organizing, and carrying out a range of activities, from fundraising events to membership drives. Many organizations and committees operate much like businesses. So, you're likely to learn a lot about budgets, public and community relations, and teamwork—even if you start out on the periphery. Highlight these experiences just as you would a paying job on your resume and in future interviews.

Are you an unpublished writer or graphic designer desperate for "ink"? This is your chance to add an organization's newsletter to your portfolio by volunteering to write free articles or design a logo "pro bono" for your uncle's new business. ("Pro bono" is a fancy way of saying for free. Advertising agencies and law firms do it regularly.)

In the process, you will no doubt capture the attention and gain the trust and admiration of other members of your organization, some of whom just may be in a position to hire you—or refer you to someone else who can.

## Classwork with class

Many of the projects you complete as part of your required coursework give you valuable experience identifying, researching, and solving problems that occur in real life. Perhaps you've designed a corporate identity program for a fictional client or maybe you designed and built a robot you can walk right into the interview! Coursework combines knowledge and creativity in a way that prospective employers will hope you'll demonstrate again on the job.

## If all else fails, make your own job

This is a gutsy move. If you're dying to show what you can do, but lack specific experience, present yourself with a challenge and show how you would solve it. If you treat this "make work" just as you would a real job assignment, prospective employers are likely to sit up and take notice. Create an original ad campaign or rework an existing media program. (Just don't present your rework to the agency that did the original work!) In the case of artists, photographers, writers, and designers who must present portfolios of finished work, this is an ideal way to develop a quality package.

If you're in another field, think of what kinds of challenges you'd like to be presented with on the job and see if a "make work" project would show off your talents to a prospective employer.

## Making your resume your project

Many new college students are finding innovative ways to show their knowledge and skills in one-of-a-kind resumes. The key here is to be appropriate. To paraphrase architects, "Form must follow function." That is, the final result should make sense and heighten the impact of the knowledge and experience you're trying to sell, not simply make an all-out attempt to grab attention. I think you'll see what I mean from the following bright ideas:

- Students in an international business program prepared their credentials in both English and Chinese.
- One young man sent out a video resume titled "Don't Make Lee Costic Move Back Home With His Parents." A sequel, "Don't Make Lee Costic Work in a Department Store," landed him a job in video graphics.
- Seniors in an environmental studies program each composed a resume/self-mailer to environmentally conscious companies. Each recycled sheet contained a cover sheet on one side and resume on the other.

Consider this: Many advertising agencies and companies are looking for people with multimedia skills. If yours are impressive or you have a portfolio of work to show a creative director, you might create an interactive resume using this technology. Again, remember that substance is more important than style. Dazzling special effects will never make up for sloppy editing and poor quality graphics. It's also a good idea to make sure that the recipient has the hardware and software necessary to view your work of art.

Inspired? Now it's time to think about and decide upon the industry, specific company, and specific job description you're seeking. The next couple of chapters will show you how to do it.

# Chapter 4

# Finding the Right Company

This chapter shifts the focus of your job search. Our previous discussion has concentrated on what *you* bring to the table—your skills and capabilities and how closely they match those required by specific career disciplines. It's time to look at companies themselves and the important factors that will help you choose between them: the job description, company profile, and corporate culture. It will become apparent how these three factors are connected and how fundamentally they affect one another. You'll also see how they affect the content and tone of your resume, as well as your approach to the interviewing process.

But before we focus on your preferences, let's start by recording what you already know.

Take a sheet of blank paper (yes, it's time for another list) and divide it into three vertical columns. Title it, "My Ideal Company Profile." Call the left-hand column, "Musts," the middle column, "Preferences," and the right-hand column, "Nevers." I've listed a series of questions below. After considering each one, decide whether a particular criteria *must* be met, whether you would *prefer* it or whether you'd *never* consider it at all. If there are other criteria you consider important, add them to the list below and mark them accordingly on your profile.

1. What are your geographical preferences? (Possible answers: the Northeastern U.S., Canada, international, anywhere.) If you only want to work in the U.S., "Work in United States" would be the entry in the "Must" column. "Work in Canada or Foreign Country" might be the first entry in your "Never" column. If, however, you will consider working in two of the three, then your "Must" column entry might read "Work in U.S. or Canada," your "Preference" entry—if you preferred one over the other—could read "Work in U.S.," and the "Never" column could read "Work Overseas."

2. Do you prefer a large city, small city, town, or somewhere as far away from civilization as possible?

3. Do you prefer a warm or cold climate?

4. Do you prefer a large or small company? Define your terms (by sales, income, employees, etc.).

5. Do you mind traveling frequently? What percentage of your time do you consider "reasonable"?

6. What salary would you like to receive (put in the "Prefeence" column)? What's the lowest salary you'll accept (in the "Must" column)?

7. Are there any benefits (such as an expense account, medical and/or dental insurance, company car, etc.) you must or would like to have?

8. Are you planning to attend graduate school at some point in the future? If so, is it important to you that a tuition reimbursement plan be part of the company benefits package?

9. What kinds of products/services/accounts would you prefer to work with?

10. Is it important that the company have a formal employee training program?

It's important to continually revise this form—after all, it contains the criteria by which you will judge every potential employer. It may even lead you to *avoid* interviewing at a specific company (if, for example, it's located in a state on your "Never" list). So be sure your "Nevers" aren't frivolous.

Likewise, make your "Musts" and "Preferences" at least semi-realistic. If your "Must" salary for an entry-level position in book publishing is $50,000, I guarantee you're barking up the wrong tree!

## Taking command

Here comes another chart, one we'll call your "Command Chart" or "Company Evaluation Chart." When completed, it will summarize all your research on the firms you've initially targeted. As you start networking, sending out resumes and cover letters, and preparing for interviews, you will find yourself constantly updating and referring to this chart.

Create one vertical column down the left side, where you'll begin listing the companies you're considering. Then, make as many columns across the top of the chart as you need to list all your "Must" and "Preference" criteria so you can "grade" them accordingly.

For example, using a list of possible entries on a hypothetical company profile, we would write in the following column headings and make an entry for each targeted firm in the appropriate space (from those possible, noted in parentheses):

1. **State.** List those you'll consider.
2. **City.** Name them.
3. **Company size.** By number of employees.
4. **Formal training program.** Check if "yes" and note important details—who's in charge, number of trainees hired each year, etc.
5. **Benefits.** List all company-wide benefits and circle those especially important to you.
6. **Travel.** Enter percentage anticipated.
7. **Salary.** You'll probably want to leave this blank until you're able to enter a specific offer, but you may want to include anything you discover about that company's general pay scales, etc.

Feel free to combine, add to, alter, and use this new chart in any way that makes sense to you. While you should set up individual files for the companies high on your list, this Command Chart will remain an important form to refer to. As we discuss new evaluation criteria later in this chapter, you may need to expand this chart accordingly.

## 40 words or less, please

Job descriptions summarize particular job functions—duties, responsibilities, and the minimal requirements, education, and skills an applicant would need to fill a position. The *Dictionary of Occupational Titles*, available in virtually every library, is a good basic reference for researching specific job titles and descriptions. (Its "companion"—the *Occupational Outlook Handbook*—will help you evaluate the industries' needs for each such job function in the next decade.) Remember: Titles may vary widely from company to company, so focus on the description.

The importance of such job descriptions should be obvious: They allow you to sort through and include or eliminate those career opportunities for which you are minimally qualified. And they can serve as a springboard for your preparation of the "Objective" section of your resume, which we'll talk about later.

They will also help you differentiate between seemingly similar job titles that, in reality, represent radically different functions—and discover seemingly different job titles that actually require the same skills and represent the same duties and responsibilities.

To give you a better idea of what you're looking for, here are some representative (and real) job titles and descriptions extracted from various company manuals:

**Employee benefits assistant**—Assist in analyzing, designing, and implementing employee benefits program under close supervision of Director of Personnel Services. Should be adept at figures and cost analysis, and possess effective written and verbal communications skills. Familiarity with liability, health, and compensation insurance helpful; familiarity with computers essential.

**Sales trainee**—Excellent communications skills. Call on customers and set up appointments from furnished leads. Good administrative follow-up, including correspondence and telemarketing activities. Responsive to structured sales approach.

**Assistant product manager**—Strong self-starter, well organized, with economics/business degree. Assist in planning and implementing functions for major software product line sold to the automotive after-market field. Packaging, pricing, competitive analysis skills required.

**Software engineer**—Degree in computer science and/or experience. Fluent in various high-level computer languages. Knowledge of word processing, graphics, image processing, relational databases. Ability to relate to non-technical personnel in a dynamic work environment.

**Advertising account trainee**—Degree in advertising, marketing, or business administration. Knowledge of survey techniques, research, budget planning, long-range planning is desirable. Good people skills, high energy level. Flexible attitude and strong written communications skills mandatory.

**Limousine chauffeur**—Perfect driving safety record: trucks, vans, public vehicles. Minimal English language reading and writing skills. Presentable, courteous, able to work long hours with considerable overtime. Familiarity with major urban, suburban geography. State motor vehicle license #4.

Obviously, these descriptions contain a great deal of valuable information. At a minimum, you should be looking for the following:

**Practical skills**—You can be certain you will not be considered unless you have them.

**Hidden skills**—For example, "people skills," where so noted. These are probably understated and might really be a very important part of the job function.

**Educational credentials**—When a certain degree or level of educational accomplishment is required, it won't help you to "fudge" if you don't have it. Rather, inquire whether work experience is an acceptable substitute.

# Read between the lines

As important as the objective resources outlined in the last chapter are, no book can tell you what it's really like to work at a specific company. So, try to find out from the inside. Your best bet is to find and interview someone who works there. This will give you practical information—from someone already doing what you *hope* to be doing. (I'll show you how to schedule and conduct such informational interviews in Chapter 6.)

Barring that avenue, the company's annual report (or company brochure) usually contains detailed descriptive data. Don't take it as gospel—it is, after all, the way the company wants its public to see it.

## Buttoned-down or blue-jeaned?

A company's physical environment, management attitude and policies, and the type of people it hires all shape a company's "culture." That culture is a key determinant affecting whether you'll enjoy your job. Here are some examples of typical corporate cultures:

### All in the family

Some companies are dominated by a single personality, either a still-active founder, or an executive who has exerted a strong, long-lasting influence on policies and style. Think Jack Welch at GE, Bill Gates at Microsoft, or Ted Turner. While there are exceptions, such companies tend to be "closely held" fiefdoms whose every level reflects the "cult of personality." If that personality is a despot, benign, or otherwise, even a decentralized management structure won't create a company everyone wants to work for. (Gates, for one, is reportedly a very difficult boss.)

Family-owned companies often pose similar problems. Your chance to make decisions and take responsibility may be tied to your last name. Barely competent family members may wind up with cushy jobs and high pay, while you and other "outsiders" do all the work. While many such firms are privately held, even publicly traded companies in which family members hold the majority of stock still answer primarily to the family.

### Politics as usual

Many larger, more decentralized companies will spread decision-making power and opportunities for advancement somewhat more evenly. However, such companies often encourage competition among workers rather than focusing collective energies against competing organizations.

If managers regularly spend half their time politicking or writing self-serving memos to the boss, it's a survival-of-the-fittest atmosphere. People attuned to corporate in-fighting might relish such a company; those who just want to do their jobs and be rewarded for the work they do will find it an unfriendly place to work.

### High energy? Low-key?

Some companies are bursting with energy. Their offices seem to reverberate with a steady hum of activity. Such a high-key environment is right for aggressive go-getters who are unafraid of such a fast pace and more than ready, even eager, to jump into the fray. Other workplaces are calmer, quiet, almost studious in nature. Such low-key firms are probably better choices for more laid-back personalities.

While a high-energy or low-key atmosphere says little about a particular company's chances for success, it may have a lot to do with your own on-the-job performance, success, and happiness. Matching dissimilar corporate and individual personalities usually results in a new job search.

If you run across a company that seems to give off no signals at all, beware! This is usually an organization without direction, one that lacks both an agenda and dynamic leadership. Without such leadership, you can be certain that this organization will flounder, usually when things start going wrong, and the timely implementation of company-wide decisions is required.

## Feeling right at home

Let's pretend for a moment: You have been hired as a draftsman for a prestigious engineering firm. Your first day on the job, several things happen almost simultaneously: 1) You are told that for your first week you will be assigned to the new employee-training sessions sponsored by the Human Resources department; 2) a multi-page folder titled "Employee Benefits and Work Policies" is dropped on your desk; and 3) you are invited to a Friday Beer Bust after work in the company cafeteria.

This is a company that obviously cares about its employees and has made a commitment to train them, care for their needs, and make them feel at home. This is the kind of corporate culture you were seeking all along. Were you just lucky you stumbled on the right fit? Not at all! You owe your good fortune to all those hours you spent researching just these kinds of details!

# Chapter 5

# Getting Help When You Need It

Take advantage of the public and private employment services in your community. These may include employment and counseling services that are part of the federal government (and most state and local governments) as well as an array of more specialized recruiters, counselors, and employment agencies in the business of helping job seekers find jobs. Estimates are that between 7 and 10 percent of all successful job searches go through these channels. Yours could be one of them.

In addition, the growth of the Internet has added a wide array of sites on which to post your resume, network, and browse job openings. While you should not limit your search to online postings, you certainly shouldn't ignore them. I'll give you an up-to-date list of the best sites later in this chapter.

## Open season on you

Employment agencies and recruiters are sometimes retained by companies to screen candidates for particular job openings. Both types of firms can be found in your local yellow pages under the headings, "Employment Agencies," "Vocational Guidance," and/or, "Executive Recruiting Firms."

How do these two types of "screening" firms differ? Employment agencies typically survive on high volume—lots of job openings in lots of industries. While many of these are entry-level opportunities, they are invariably clerical or secretarial. (Most get their fees from the companies, not from you.) If that's the kind of position you are seeking, your local employment agency should be a first stop.

If you are hoping for a position that has more potential to lead you up the career ladder, the executive recruiter, who plays a more discriminating role for his or her client companies, is your best bet. Recruiting firms often specialize in a single industry.

Since recruiters generally charge their client companies a higher fee than general employment agencies, companies tend to use them for harder-to-fill executive slots. Of course, there are always exceptions, and you would be advised to at least inquire at any local recruiting firms for potential openings that require little or no experience. You can get a list of recruiting firms by writing for a copy of the *Executive Employment Guide*, available from the American Management Association (135 West 50th St., New York, NY 10020). If you have or are earning an M.B.A., get a copy of the *M.B.A. Employment Guide* (Association of M.B.A. Executives, 227 Commerce St., East Haven, CT 06512).

If you plan to work with either type of firm, make sure you:

- **Don't just saunter into a local employment agency or recruiter.** Ask a friend or acquaintance that has already found employment through the organization to refer you. The networking skills you'll develop in the next chapter will surely help you here.

- **Work with only one organization in each industry.** If a company receives your resume from three different agencies, it is already apparent to them that you are "shotgunning" the field—just hoping to hit a target, any target. It's much better to give the impression that you are a selective, targeted job hunter that knows what he or she wants.

- **Try to establish a close relationship with the organization and individual with whom you work.** If she gets you a job, and you turn out to be successful at it, rest assured that you'll be on her list for future opportunities. And if you refer friends and colleagues to her, you will have established an important debt—she'll owe you!

## Let your fingers do the walking

The remainder of this chapter will review a host of sources you can access to get the job lead information you need. But don't overlook the most obvious source of all—your local telephone directory. While it will not be quite as overwhelming as the Manhattan Yellow Pages—which features more than two dozen pages of listings just for employment agencies—I suspect you'll be surprised at the number of helpful offices you'll find. It's a start.

## Let the search begin!

Down to the nitty-gritty—a listing and assessment of the most valuable resources that can be found in most cities. If you live in a major city— New York, Los Angeles, or Dallas, for example—the facilities available to you will be greater in number and scope than if you live in a small town. So, if you are a small-town resident, it would be worth a few calls, even a trip or two, to the largest metropolitan center in your area.

## State employment agencies

Most state laws mandate that these offices make all job openings known to everyone. You'll find them displayed on their office bulletin boards.

State civil service jobs offered might also be advertised in specialty publications available at local newsstands. Most competitive-examination job openings are also listed in such periodicals. A friend of mine who landed a position as a state Public Information Officer learned of the position through such a listing.

State unemployment/outplacement centers are also sources of job leads—many good job openings are in their computer files. Savvy employers know that many people who are unemployed are in that condition through no fault of their own and are anxiously seeking work. They place a high value on this pool of talent, especially since they don't have to pay private agency fees.

You usually do not have to be receiving unemployment benefits to qualify or apply for such jobs. Ask for more information at the unemployment office in your area.

## Job information centers

Since you should be spending a lot of time in your local library anyway, researching the different industries, companies, and job functions you're interested in, the next time you're there, see if they have a section that acts as a job clearing center.

## Human services agencies

As the federal government continues to decrease its role in the delivery of social services, many states, counties, and cities, as well as private groups, have taken over such efforts.

Send inquiries to the headquarters of the human services or social services organizations in each city you're interested in for a list of women's groups, social service organizations, rehabilitation centers, and support associations that might offer job search assistance.

## Veterans' organizations

If you qualify, you can get a good deal of job information (and preferential treatment because of your status) through these centers. The Veterans Administration (based in Washington, D.C.) can give you a list of federally funded branches and information on privately funded veterans groups in your city or area.

And don't forget your local chapters of the American Legion or Veterans of Foreign Wars (VFW).

## College/high school placement offices

If you are a college graduate—or plan to be one soon—by all means, take advantage of the career counseling, job placement, or career resource center at your school. Employers are always in touch with them. Some actively recruit on campus.

If you are interested in a particular company that is scheduling an on-campus visit, get in touch with the advisor at your college and make sure you get on the interview list.

The help available through high school guidance offices is often more limited, as a good part of their effort is directed to students going to college. Opportunities for high school graduates are becoming scarcer every day, though many employers still target the graduates of vocational, clerical, and trade schools.

## Community and junior colleges

These schools have become particularly valuable to certain employers because they produce candidates whose skills and interests are highly targeted. Companies specializing in technical products and services, such as computers or technical training, usually don't require their employees to have a mastery of English literature or medieval history. Rather than scout out graduates of four-year colleges, they are likely to stay in close contact with two-year colleges in their local areas.

## Trade, technical, and business schools

Secretarial, bartending, barber, beauty, TV repair, computer programming, and trade schools offer specialized training and job placement. Most good schools in these specialties are probably worth the tuition. Before you pay your money, though, make sure you check out each trade school you're considering with the local Better Business Bureau. While virtually all four- and two-year colleges are accredited, there have been more than enough instances of "fly-by-night" trade institutions to make a smart consumer pause before forking over the sometimes hefty tuition.

It's a good idea to get a second opinion from the company or companies you've targeted for future employment. If they make it a practice to hire graduates from a particular school, you should probably be enrolling there.

## Trade associations and publications

Virtually every industry, and even most specialized job functions, now have their own associations, each of which usually publishes magazines, journals, and newsletters. A local chapter of the association itself is a terrific place to network, and the publications often include job listings (though not necessarily a plethora of entry-level positions).

*Job fairs and recruiting visits*

The latter is probably a better place to do some serious networking than the former, but only if you're at a college that actively solicits and supports such visits.

Job fairs are far less targeted and better attended—you'll be competing with thousands of other hopefuls for face time, especially at the "hot" companies. Most are free. At worst, they're a good opportunity to meet a lot of recruiters in a single day. At best, you may find exactly the company you've been searching for. Check out *www.jobfairdates.com* for listings of upcoming job fairs in your area.

## Dealing with bureaucracies

Here are some time-tested tips to keep in mind as you prepare to deal with the employment bureaucracy:

- **Be proactive in your dealings with your counselor.** Government personnel all too often work by the book. Limited incentive and restrictive disciplinary practices can be corrosive to performance. So, if you think the person you are dealing with is doing the absolute minimum and offering nothing if not asked—repeatedly—he or she probably is. The trick is to know what each organization has to offer and how to work with each personality type you encounter to take full advantage of the resources.

- **Be courteous.** There might well be a good deal of tedium and routine in the jobs that these people are asked to do. A smile and a good word may make their day—and provide an incentive for them to make yours by promptly giving you the information you require.

- **Be persistent.** If you don't get the information you need the first time around, don't be afraid to go back and/or try another person in the same office. There is a considerable amount of shifting of such personnel and an abundance of part-time help (who may know the location of the rest rooms, but little else!). If you are sure the answer you require lurks somewhere in that office, keep searching for the person who knows it and keep asking until you get it.

- **Avoid the fast-acting, fill-the-job personality types.** Whether they are counselors at employment agencies or recruiters, they are rarely concerned about your objectives, only about what (or who) they can sell to a prospective employer. These are the "body snatcher/headhunter" types you may already have heard about. Value the recruiter or agent that displays a genuine interest in you.

# Online services

This resource cannot be overlooked as a convenient and relatively economical way to locate (and be located by) companies and recruiters who are hiring.

There are currently a multitude of bulletin boards, databases, and specialized online services specifically geared to matching prospective candidates with companies that are hiring. Most contain job listings posted by employers that job seekers can respond to online or via regular mail. Some play matchmaker, actively matching the resumes or career profiles of job seekers with available openings posted by their client companies.

What's more, by posting your resume online, you can be in front of corporate hiring managers and recruiters 24 hours a day, seven days a week, 365 days a year.

Metajob boards are the most wide-ranging places to start, since they allow you to search hundreds, even thousands, of job sites all at once. Three of the most popular are *careerbuilder.com* (which searches 75 sites), *employment911.com* (which boasts 3 million job listings and searches 350 job sites) *jobsearchengine.com* (which searches 300 sites in the U.S. and Canada). Most metajob sites allow you to post a resume and create a personalized job search that features e-mail notification of new job postings that meet your criteria (as do many of the individual job sites listed below).

According to Rebecca Smith, best-selling author of *Electronic Resumes and Online Networking, 2nd Edition* (Career Press, 2000), the top ten job search sites, compiled by Media Matrix, based on unique monthly visits, are:

- *www.monster.com*
- *www.careermosaic.com* (now part of *headhunter.net*)
- *www.careerpath.com* (now part of *careerbuilder.com*)
- *www.jobsearch.org*
- *www.headhunter.net*
- *www.nationjob.com*
- *www.hotjobs.com*
- *www.nettemps.com*
- *www.dice.com*
- *www.careerbuilder.com*

Two of her other picks deserve mention: For high tech jobs, she recommends *computerjobs.com*. And for freelance jobs, *guru.com*.

In addition to these more general sites, Rebecca recommends the following specifically for college graduates:

- *www.recruitinglinks.com* (search by location, industry and job function)
- *www.careerhighway.com*
- *www.jobdirect.com* (all entry-level jobs)

- *www.jobtrak.com* (works with more than 1,100 college career centers across the country; now part of Monster.com)
- *www.mbanetwork.com* (links to more than 700 recruiters inteested in MBAs)
- *www.careerpark.com*
- *www.recruitersonline.com* (more than 8,000 registered recruiters)
- *www.alumni-network.com* (job openings for experienced and new grads in high tech)

This is the merest sampling of the informational smorgasbord available online. In addition, there are even more targeted sites to check out if you are disabled *(www.hirediversity.com)*, fluent in Spanish or Portugese *(www.latpro.com)*, or just interested in working in a particular state (individual sites for each state, plus, in many cases, numerous cities and colleges, all offering job openings!) The list of Web-based resources is virtually endless. You'll find the Internet helpful during virtually every step of the job search process.

In addition to job listings, you can track down sometimes obscure information to impress a prospective employer in an interview, or chat with someone who can provide inside information about an industry or employer. You can even get online career coaching through virtually any of the major job search sites.

Anyone who can master the Internet is likely to know something about word processing, spreadsheets, or database searches—knowledge required for most good jobs these days. If this isn't you—yet—your local librarian can guide you through the online offerings.

# Chapter 6

# You Heard It Through the Grapevine?

Networking is the process of turning to relatives, friends, and acquaintances to feed you the information you need to find a job—identifying where the jobs are and giving you the background data and personal introductions necessary to pursue them.

While the term networking didn't gain prominence until the 1970s, it is by no means a new phenomenon. A selection process that connects people of similar skills, backgrounds, and/or attitudes—in other words, networking—has been in existence in one form or another for centuries.

Attend any Ivy League school, for example, and you're automatically part of its very special networkthat is centuries old.

A so-called Old Boys Network has been at work in this country for years, especially in the selection of Presidential candidates (not to mention Chairmen, CEOs, and other high flyers). What else can explain why a single New England prep school can boast of a disproportionate number of Oval Office inhabitants from among its alumni?

Major law firms are known to favor candidates from a preferred list of law schools—typically, the same ones the senior partners attended. Washington, D.C. and Corporate America have their own networks. And very often, networks overlap, like the ones that allow corporate bigwigs to move back and forth from the boardroom to the Cabinet Room.

Most importantly, networking works, because it's based on a decidedly human prejudice—the desire to "fit in" with a group. In a way, it's a built-in screening process.

If the job market were so well organized that details on all employment opportunities were immediately available to all applicants, there would be no need for such a process. Rest assured that the job market is not such a smooth-running machine, even with the democratizing rise of Internet job sites. Most applicants are still left very much on their own. Build and use your own network wisely, and you'll be amazed at the amount of useful job intelligence it will uncover.

# Creating the ideal network

The following tips will help you identify and expand your own wide-ranging, information-gathering, interview-generating group—your network:

1.  **Diversify.** Unlike the Harvard or Princeton networks, which are confined to graduates of those schools, your network should be as diversified and wide-ranging as possible. You never know who might be able to help, so don't limit your contacts to just relatives and close friends. The wider you cast your net, the more kinds of fish you'll catch.

2.  **Include everybody.** Your initial networking list should include just about every living, breathing person you know—friends, relatives, social acquaintances, classmates, college alumni, professors, teachers, dentists, doctors, family lawyers, insurance agents, bankers, travel agents, elected officials in your community, clergy, fellow members of your house of worship, local trades people, local business owners, and social club officers. And everybody *they* know!

3.  **Make specific requests.** Calling everyone and simply asking for "whatever help you can give me" is unfair to the people you're calling—and not very effective. Instead, make a list of the kinds of assistance you'll need from the people in your network. Then make specific requests of each person. Do they know of jobs at their company? Can they introduce you to the proper executives? Have they heard something about or know someone at the company you're planning to interview with next week? The more organized you are, the easier it will be to figure out who might have the information you need.

4.  **Value your contacts.** Keep those who have provided helpful information or introductions informed about how it all turns out. Such courtesy will be appreciated and may lead to more contacts. If someone you call has nothing to offer today, make a note to yourself to call back in a few months.

5.  **Maintain detailed records.** Keep your options open and your contact list alive. Detailed records of your network—with whom you spoke, when, what transpired, etc.—will help you keep track of your overall progress and organize what can be a highly complicated process.

# Information *only*

There is a huge difference between a job interview (which comes much later) and an informational interview (which I'm going to prepare you for right now). In an informational interview, information is the only thing you're after—information that you hope will someday get you a job, but that's *someday*. Right now, you are the interviewer. Your goal is to learn as much as possible about the industry, company, and job you've targeted.

A meeting with someone already doing what you soon *hope* to be doing is by far the best way to find out what you need to know *before* a formal job interview. You'll find that most people are happy to talk about their jobs. I know I often sit down with "friends of friends" and share what I've learned about book publishing. Because there is no immediate pressure on me to evaluate that "friend" as a candidate, I can be more informal, forthcoming, and relaxed.

If you learn of a specific job opening during an informational interview, you are in a position to find out many important details about it. You may also identify the actual interviewer and, if you're lucky, gain some valuable insight into her experience and personality. With your contact's permission, you may also be able to use his name as a referral.

That can really warm up a cold call. "Joan Smith in your New Accounts department suggested I contact you regarding the opening for an assistant bank teller. Can you give me some information about the position?" is significantly stronger than, "Hello. Can you give me some information about any job openings?"

## What it's all about

As you prepare to conduct informational interviews, there are, ideally, six individual goals you hope to fulfill during each:

1. To unearth current information about the industry, company and pertinent job functions. Remember: Gaining knowledge and understanding of broad industry trends, financial health of the industry and its key players, hiring opportunities, and the competitive picture are key components in your search for the right job.
2. To investigate each company's hiring policies: Who makes the decisions? Who are the key players? Is there a hiring season?
3. To sell yourself and leave a calling card, your resume.
4. To seek out advice to help you refine your job search.
5. To obtain referrals that can give you additional information.
6. To develop a list of follow-up activities that will heighten your visibility among your key contacts.

## Laying the foundation

You were, of course, smart enough to include Mike Swantic, the bank officer who handled your dad's mortgage, on your original contact list. He knew you as a bright and conscientious college senior. In fact, your perfect three- year repayment record on the loan you took out to buy that '67 Plymouth impressed him. When you called him, he was happy to refer you to his friend, Dennis Bartlett, Chief Financial Officer at XYZ Corp.

Armed with permission to use Swantic's name and recommendation, you wrote a letter to Mr. Bartlett, something like this:

*I am writing at the suggestion of Mr. Swantic at Fidelity National Bank. He knows of my interest in corporate finance and, given your position at XYZ, thought you might be able to help me get a clearer understanding of the field, as well as how I might eventually be able to obtain a job with a good company.*

*While I am taking advanced courses in finance and economics, I know I need to speak with professionals like you to get a better understanding of the big picture. If you could spare a few moments to meet with me, I'm certain I would be able to gather enough information to give me the direction I need.*

*I'll call your office next week so we can schedule a meeting.*

By sending a copy of your letter to Mr. Swantic at the bank, you made sure he would be prepared should Mr. Bartlett call to inquire about you.

## Making contact

Now you're ready for the next step: the follow-up phone call. After you get Mr. Bartlett's secretary on the line, it will, with luck, go something like this:

**You:** "Hello, I'm Kristen Hamilton. I'm calling in reference to a letter I wrote to Mr. Bartlett requesting an appointment."

**Secretary:** "Oh, yes. You're the young woman majoring in finance and economics. Mr. Bartlett can see you on June 23rd at 10 a.m."

**You:** "That's fine. I'll be there. Thank you very much"

## The interview

On the appointed day, you—well-scrubbed and dressed in your best (and most conservative) suit, of course—are ushered into Mr. Bartlett's office. The conversation might go something like this:

**You:** "Thank you for seeing me, Mr. Bartlett. I know you are busy, and I appreciate your taking the time to talk with me."

**Bartlett:** "Well, it's my pleasure since you come so highly recommended. I'm always pleased to meet someone interested in this field."

**You:** "As I stated in my letter, my interest in finance is very real, but I'm having trouble seeing how all of my studies fit into the big picture. I think I'll be much better prepared to evaluate future job offers if I can learn how everything fits. May I ask you a few questions about the finance function at your company?"

At this point, Mr. Bartlett relaxes. He has been assured you really are just seeking advice and information, not ensnaring him into a thinly veiled job interview. Your approach has let him off the hook—he doesn't have to be concerned with making a hiring decision today. You've already gotten high marks for not putting him on the defensive.

**Bartlett:** "Fire away, Kristen."

**You:** "I have a few specific questions I'd like to ask. First, how is the finance function organized?"

**Bartlett:** "In this company, we work on a centralized basis. All operating departments funnel their requests for expenditures to us—all of their invoices and budgets must pass through Finance."

**You:** "Do you feel this limits the opportunities for career advancement into other areas of the company?"

**Bartlett:** "Good question! No, we make a special effort to see that all personnel understand the functions of each of our departments. Many people from Finance wind up in Administration."

**You:** "What is your opinion about the corporate finance field in general, and what do you see as the most likely areas of opportunity in the foreseeable future? Do you think this is a growth area?"

**Bartlett:** "Judging by our hiring record, I think you'll find it's an area worth making a commitment to, particularly in global finance. As you may already know, it is really exploding."

**You:** "How would someone with my qualifications and background get started in this area? Perhaps a look at my resume would be helpful to you."

At this point, you pass your resume to Mr. Bartlett.

**Bartlett:** "We start our entry-level employees in Accounting, then we move them into other areas, such as Treasury. I think these courses you've taken would more than qualify you for such a position."

**You:** "You have been very generous with your time, but I can see from those flashing buttons on your phone that you have other things to do. Are there other people at XYZ, or in the industry, you think I should talk with?"

## After the interview

The next step should be obvious. *Two* thank-you letters are required—one to Mr. Bartlett, the second to Mr. Swantic. Get them both written and mailed *immediately*. (See Chapter 11 for help writing them.)

What now? Cross this contact off your master list and move on? If you do, you'll certainly have wasted a lot of effort, and you might be forfeiting some valuable future opportunities.

## Keeping track so you can keep in touch

Experts have estimated that the average person could develop a contact list of 250 people. Even if we limit your initial list to only 50, if each of your initial contacts gives you just one referral, your list will have grown to 100 names in no time. Therefore, it is essential to keep accurate records.

Get the results of each interview down on paper and create a file called, "Interview Recap Record." Record the following information on an index card, in a notebook or, ideally, on a computer database. It should be set up something like this:

**Name:** XYZ Company

**Address:** 22 Sheridan Place, Elmira, NY 14902

**Phone:** (607) 555-8291

**Contact:** Dennis L. Bartlett

**Type of Business:** Aircraft Engine Manufacturer

**Referral Contact:** Michael Swantic, Fidelity National Bank

**Date:** September 23, 2001

**Results:** At this point, you should add a one- or two-paragraph summary of what you found out at the meeting. State the facts (what you found out in response to your specific questions), as well as your *impressions* (your assessment of the opportunities for further discussions, your "gut feeling" about your chances of being considered for future openings). Based on your interview with XYZ Corp., you might include the following:

> XYZ looks to college-trained personnel to fill its entry-level finance slots. Operations are centralized. Company emphasizes full employee understanding of all facets of operations and encourages interdepartmental transfers. Work environment is low-key. Finance is seen as a growth area based on the company's prior hiring record and the growing importance of global trade. Mr. Bartlett seemed impressed with my resume and general presentation. I could tell from the pictures on his office wall that he is an outdoors type.

## Out of sight, out of mind...

That's just what you *don't* want to be. So, take advantage of any logical opportunities to stay in touch with Mr. Bartlett. You may, for example, let him know when you graduate, copy him on letters to Mr. Swantic or to any of the contacts he gave you, even clip a pertinent article from the local paper about his department and send it to him with a note. This type of follow-up will keep you on his radar screen. No matter how talented you may be or how good an impression you made, you'll have to work hard to "stay visible."

## Turning the tables

Of course, the line between the people who can give you information about a certain field you've targeted and potential employers in that field can sometimes blur. Don't be concerned—you'll soon learn when (and how) to shift the focus from interview*er* to interview*ee*.

To simplify this process, follow a single rule: Show interest in the industry or job area under discussion, but wait to be asked about actually working for that company. During your informational interviews, you will be surprised at how often the person you're interviewing turns to you and asks, "Would you be interested in _____?" If you *would* be interested in the position under discussion, by all means make your feelings known.

## Six good reasons to network

Many people shy away from the networking process because they think they are "bothering" other people with their own selfish demands. Nonsense! There are at least half a dozen excellent reasons the people in your network will be happy to help you:

1. **Someday you'll return the favor.** An ace insurance salesman built a successful business by offering low-cost coverage to first-year medical students. Ten years later, these now-successful practitioners remembered the company (and the salesman) that helped them when they were just getting started. He gets new referrals every day.

2. **They need you just as much as you need them.** If you sense that your "brain is being picked" about the latest techniques of computer graphics, be forthcoming with your information. Schools and universities are often at the forefront of technology, so why not let the interviewer "audit" your course? It may be the reason he or she agreed to see you in the first place.

3. **You make them look important.** Internal politics can be a powerful motivator. Some people will see you simply to make themselves appear powerful, implying to others in their organization that they have the authority to hire.

4. **They know it's better to be safe than sorry.** Nobody knows better than today's hiring managers how quickly things can change. Someone may give notice tomorrow. A new client may stretch staff resources to the limits. By maintaining a

backlog of qualified candidates, they can move quickly to hire the best people.

5. **They've been in your shoes.** Some people will see you simply because they know how you feel. They've been there, and they feel that "giving back" is the decent thing to do.

6. **They want to keep their own "net" working.** Most people are anxious to do a friend (whoever referred you) a favor. If a colleague is seeking new talent, you might represent a referral. You see, networking never really stops—it helps them, and it helps you.

Before you proceed to Chapter 7, begin making your contact list. You may wish to keep a separate sheet of paper or note card on each person (especially the dozen or so you think are most important). You might even want to compile a separate telephone list to make your communications easier and more efficient. However you set up your list, be sure to keep it up-to-date. It won't be long before you'll be calling each and every number.

## Down to the nitty-gritty

At last, it's time to go on to the reason you bought this book in the first place: learning how to prepare your resume. The detailed research you have accomplished, the skills you have begun to develop, and the exhausting prep-aratory work you have undertaken have created the foundation for your job search process. They are the brick and mortar that will make these latter steps seem almost easy. You've already done the hard work.

So sharpen your pencil, and let's finally start using all that research you've done to make a resume.

# Chapter 7

# You're Almost Ready to Write Your Resume

Before you can actually write your resume, you must assemble and organize all the personal, educational, and employment data from which you will choose the pieces that actually end up on paper. If this material is properly organized, writing a resume is a relatively seamless process, simply a matter of transforming information from one format (the record-keeping sheets in this chapter) to another (the resume formats in the next chapter).

But there *is* a lot of information you're going to be organizing, so the first step is to designate a single location in which to store all your records. Losing important report cards, transcripts, citations, letters, etc. is all-too-easy to do if your life's history is scattered about your room or, even worse, throughout your house. I suggest keeping separate file folders for each major segment of information.

Here's what your record-keeping system should include:

## Report cards, transcripts, and licenses

Transcripts are your school's official record of your academic history, usually available, on request, from your high school guidance counselor's or college registrar's office. Your school-calculated Grade Point Average (GPA) should be on the transcript. Some (not all) may include your class rank. These latter two numbers are important, so if they are not on your transcript (and the latter probably won't be), get them.

In general, plan to include your GPA on your resume if it was 3.5 or higher on a 4.0 point scale or 5.0 or higher on a 6.0 scale. Be sure to indicate the scale (e.g., 3.5/4.0). If you graduated with honors, please note it, but then omit your GPA; it's redundant. If your class ranking would appear more impressive than your GPA, use the former.

There are forms on page 69 to list all your educational data, including high school, college and graduate work, vocational training, on-the-job training, licenses and certifications.

If you're in college, most of your high school records will not be relevant, but gather them anyway, especially the positive ones. If you're in graduate school, none of your high school records are needed. If you have not yet graduated, list your anticipated date of graduation. If it's more than a year away, indicate the number of credits earned through the most recent semester or quarter. If you are a recent high school, trade school, or college graduate, or have yet to graduate, you may list completed courses, but only those that apply to the position or field in which you're interested. If you've graduated and took some courses that are not related to your degree, but are specific to a new career goal, go ahead and profile them. If you worked for a period of time and are now reentering the work force after a long break, most, if not all, of your college grades are no longer relevant (though particular honors, awards, and skills may still be pertinent).

It's important to list any licenses or certifications to show the employer you're trained for the job, especially if you're in a skilled trade, such as an airline mechanic or dental assistant. Use the form on page 73.

## Employment, internship, and volunteer records

You will need the following information for every part-time or full-time job you have held. That includes internships—paid, unpaid, or for class credit. Although the information will be recorded, utilized and presented differently, you'll need exactly the same details for any volunteer activities (again, paid or unpaid). I've included separate worksheets for employment and volunteer data on pages 65-68:

- Name, address, telephone number
- Name of supervisor
- Exact dates worked (or involved)
- Approximate number of hours per week
- Specific duties and responsibilities
- Specific skills utilized
- Accomplishments
- Honors
- Copies of awards
- Letters of recommendation

Write one- or two-sentence paragraphs describing what you did at each job. For example, if you worked as a hostess in a restaurant, this section might read: "Responsible for the delivery of 250 meals at dinner time and the supervision of 20 waiters and busboys. Coordinated reservations. Responsible for check and payment verification."

When describing your skills, enumerate specific capabilities that were either necessary to get the job or that you developed while you were in it.

If you can quantify specific results—e.g., "developed new filing system," "collected more than $5,000 in previously assumed bad debt," "instituted award-winning art program," etc.—make sure you play them up. Likewise, if you received any award, citation, or other honor—"named Employee of the Month three times," "received Mayor's Citation for Innovation," etc.—make sure you list these.

Do not underestimate the pertinence of volunteer experience. Did you plan and lead meetings? Organize and supervise your sorority's annual fundraiser? Coordinate a number of volunteers? Secure sponsors to help defray costs? Raise a significant amount of money? Sounds like some pretty good resume material to me!

Co-op work experience while still in college and any experiences as a foreign exchange student are also worth noting. While the latter may not be related to your career goal, studying abroad will show you enjoyed a challenge and were willing to try new experiences.

Prepare one sheet for each job you have held, no matter how short its duration (yes, summer jobs count) or how limited you may think it is. Feel free to photocopy the forms in this book as needed.

## Activities, clubs, memberships, and hobbies

List all sports, clubs, or other activities in which you've participated, either inside or outside of school. Include your hobbies here. Even if you do not plan to list certain activities on your resume—such as those that are political or religious in nature—include them on these forms. For each, you should list:

- Name of activity/club/group
- Office(s) held
- Purpose of club/group
- Specific duties/responsibilities
- Achievements, accomplishments, awards, honors

## Honors and awards

Even if previously listed, separately record specific data on every honor and award, and, of course, store the award itself. List those from school (including prestigious high school awards, whatever your age), community groups, church groups, clubs, volunteer activities, military service, etc. Keep the following information in an awards folder:

- Name
- Date and from whom received
- What it was for
- Any pertinent details

## Specific skills & talents

Whether you can type like a demon, surf the Net with abandon, speak seven languages or are a scratch golfer, any and every skill or talent you possess should be detailed on the forms on page 73. For each, include:
- Description of skill
- Specific training in it
- Years of experience
- Level of expertise
- Accomplishments related to it

# Military service records

If pertinent, include the following details on the form on page 72:
- Branch and dates of service
- Final rank awarded
- Duties and responsibilities
- Awards and citations
- Details of special training and/or schooling
- Specific skills developed
- Specific accomplishments

A military stint can teach you many useful skills and often hastens the maturation process, making you a more attractive candidate. So if you have served in the military, make sure you collect all the pertinent information.

While you should use the forms on the following pages to summarize all the data you have collected, do not throw away any specific information—report cards, transcripts, citations, etc.—just because you've already recorded the information on these sheets. Keep *all* records in your files. You may need them again!

At this point, don't worry about the relevance of any particular item. It's highly unlikely you will include all the information you have collected on your resume, even if you're a high school student looking for your first summer job. But you can't choose what to *omit* until you have collected all the information you may want to *include*.

# 1. Work Experience

Make one copy of this worksheet for each paid job or professional internship position you have held.

1. Name of company _____
2. Address and phone number _____
_____

3. Your job title (use the actual title that would be on employee records)
_____
_____
_____

4. Start and end dates (month and year) _____
5. Salary (beginning and end) _____
6. Supervisor's name and title _____
7. General job description (one or two sentence summary) _____
_____
_____
_____

8. Responsibility
Management/supervisory duties (include size of staff and specific duties—hiring, training, etc.)_____
_____
_____
_____
_____

Budgetary/financial duties (include any duties related to money— writing a budget, totaling daily receipts, analyzing cost/profit ratios, etc.)
_____
_____
_____
_____

Sales/marketing duties (include specifics about product sold, type of customer base, advertising responsibility, long-term marketing planning, etc.)
_____
_____
_____
_____
_____

Customer service (include number of customers you served on a regular basis, plus their status—retail customer, executive-level clients, etc.)

_____

_____

_____

_____

_____

Production duties (include amount of goods/services produced on a daily, monthly, or annual basis)_____

_____

_____

_____

_____

_____

Technical duties (any duties that required you to use computers or other technical equipment)_____

_____

_____

_____

_____

_____

9. Accomplishments (including honors and awards)

_____

_____

_____

_____

_____

10. Special skills learned (computer skills, telephone sales, desktop publishing, etc.)_____

_____

_____

_____

_____

_____

_____

## 2. Volunteer Experience

Make one copy of this worksheet for each volunteer activity

1. Name of organization _____

2. Address and telephone number _____

_____

3.Position/title (if no position held, simply indicate "member")

_____

4. Start and end dates of this position _____

5. Start and end dates of your membership (month and year) _____

6. Hours devoted per week _____

7. Names of organization president(s) or your ranking superior

_____

_____

8. General description (one or two sentence summary)

_____

_____

_____

9. Responsibilites

Management/supervisory duties (include size of staff and specific duties—hiring, training, etc.)_____

_____

_____

_____

Budgetary/financial duties (include any duties related to money— writing a budget, totaling daily receipts, analyzing cost/profit ratios, etc.)

_____

_____

_____

Sales/marketing duties (include specifics about product sold, type of customer base, advertising responsibilities, long-term marketing planning, etc.)_____

_____

_____

_____

Customer service (include number of customers you served on a regular basis, plus their status—retail customer, executive-level clients, etc.)

_____

_____

_____

_____

_____

Production duties (include amount of goods/services produced on a daily, monthly, or annual basis) _____

_____

_____

_____

_____

_____

Technical duties (any duties that required you to use computers or other technical equipment)_____

_____

_____

_____

_____

_____

10. Accomplishments (including honors and awards)

_____

_____

_____

_____

11. Special skills learned (computer skills, telephone sales, desktop publishing, etc.) _____

_____

_____

_____

_____

_____

_____

_____

# 3. Education

## High school education

(If you have many years of experience under your belt, you need only complete questions 1-6 for high school education)

1. School name _____
2. Address (city and state) _____
_____
3. Years attended _____
4. Year graduated _____
5. GPA/class rank _____
6. Honors (valedictorian, top 10 percent, scholarship recipient, etc.)
_____
_____
7. Accomplishments _____
_____
8. Major courses _____
_____
9. Special skills learned _____
_____
_____

## Post-secondary education

(Make a copy for each college, tradeschool, and postgraduate institution)

1. School name _____
2. Address (city and state) _____
_____
3. Years attended _____
4. Year graduated and degree earned _____
5. GPA/ class rank _____
6. Honors (valedictorian, scholarship recipient, etc.) _____
_____
7. Accomplishments _____
_____
_____
8. Major courses _____
_____
_____
9. Special skills learned _____
_____
_____

# 4. Other Training

List any additional vocational courses, on-job training, licenses, or certification.

1. Training recieved/license or certification earned _____

_____

2. Name of training institution _____

3. Address and phone number _____

_____

4. Name and title of instructor _____

5. Skills learned _____

_____

_____

6. Accomplishments _____

_____

_____

1. Training recieved/license or certification earned _____

_____

2. Name of training institution _____

3. Address and phone number _____

_____

4. Name and title of instructor _____

5. Skills learned _____

_____

_____

6. Accomplishments _____

_____

1. Training recieved/license or certification earned _____

_____

2. Name of training institution _____

3. Address and phone number _____

_____

4. Name and title of instructor _____

5. Skills learned _____

_____

6. Accomplishments _____

_____

## 5. Honors and Awards

1. Name of award, citation, etc. _____

_____

2. From whom received _____

3. Date _____

4. Significance _____

_____

_____

5. Other pertinent information _____

_____

_____

1. Name of award, citation, etc. _____

_____

2. From whom received _____

3. Date _____

4. Significance: _____

_____

_____

5. Other pertinent information _____

_____

_____

_____

1. Name of award, citation, etc. _____

_____

2. From whom received _____

3. Date _____

4. Significance _____

_____

_____

5. Other pertinent information _____

_____

_____

_____

# 6. Activities, Clubs, Memberships, and Hobbies

1. Club/activity _____
2. Offices held _____
3. Description of participation _____
_____
4. Duties/responsibilities _____
_____
_____
5. Dates: _____

1. Club/activity _____
2. Offices held _____
3. Description of participation _____
_____
4. Duties/responsibilities _____
_____
_____
5. Dates _____

1. Club/activity _____
2. Offices held _____
3. Description of participation _____
_____
4. Duties/responsibilities _____
_____
_____
5. Dates _____

# 7. Military Service

1. Branch _____
2. Rank (at discharge) _____
3. Dates of service _____
4. Duties and responsibilities _____
_____
5. Special training and/or school attended _____
_____
6. Citations, awards, etc. _____
_____
7. Specific accomplishments _____
_____
_____

# 8. Special Skills (including Languages)

1. Name of skill _____
2. Specific training received _____
_____
_____
_____

3. Years of experience _____
4. Level of expertise _____
5. Accomplishments related to this skill _____
_____
_____
_____

1. Name of skill _____
2. Specific training received _____
_____
_____
_____

3. Years of experience _____
4. Level of expertise _____
5. Accomplishments related to this skill _____
_____
_____
_____

1. Name of skill _____
2. Specific training received _____
_____
_____
_____

3. Years of experience _____
4. Level of expertise _____
5. Accomplishments related to this skill _____
_____
_____
_____
_____
_____
_____
_____

# Chapter 8

# Constructing Your First Resume

Two hundred words. That's all that stands right now between you and a finished resume. Hardly a daunting task for someone who's written half a dozen term papers or so during your academic career.

But what words those must be! You must choose them as carefully as a poet or someone writing a new advertising slogan to premier on Super Bowl Sunday, because, as I've stressed before, your resume is a one- or two-page summary of your education, skills, employment experience, and career objective(s). It is not a biography, but a concise way to identify and describe you to potential employers. Most importantly, it might be the best hope you have of getting a job.

Assembling the information sheets in the last chapter probably has set your mind abuzz with ideas for a killer resume. Again, I suggest patience. The reason this time: There's more than one way to write a resume. Let's take a look at some of the rules you should follow and those you can bend.

## Choose the right format

For an entry-level job applicant with limited work experience, the *chronological* format, which organizes your educational and employment history by date, is the obvious choice. For older or more experienced applicants, either the *functional* format—which emphasizes the duties and responsibilities of all your jobs throughout your career—or *combination* format—a bit of chronological and functional—may be more suitable. The next chapter contains examples of all of these.

## 18 tips for the best-looking resume

1. **Limit it to one or two pages.** There was a time—not that long ago—when many career experts preached no resume should exceed a single page. For first timers, that still

shouldn't pose much of a problem! If you're a student with little or no "real world" experience, even *you* may have enough educational credentials, volunteer work, internships and summer/after school jobs to make a one-page resume way too cluttered. Don't eliminate vital information just to keep your resume to a single page. But never use more than two. Employers are looking for, among other qualities, strong organizational and communication skills. If you can't sum up your qualifications in two pages or less, they'll pass you by.

2.  **Print the word "continued" at the bottom of the first page of a two-page resume**…and put your name and "page 2" at the top of the second page. If the pages become separated—a not uncommon occurrence—someone will (hopefully) notice and (hopefully) reattach them.

3.  **Use a serif typeface** (such as the one used in this book), the kind with finials and "doodads" on all the letters. Tests show people find these typefaces easier to read, which is probably why most, if not all, of your textbooks use serif type. New Century Schoolbook, Palatino, Bookman, Times, Courier, and Souvenir are examples of basic serif typefaces.

4.  **Stick to traditional typefaces**, like those just noted. You probably have a veritable treasure trove of type on your hard drive or available on CD-ROM, but that doesn't mean a resume is the proper place to try out a typeface that is too fancy or cutesy. When in doubt, opt for readability over style.

5.  **Select a readable size.** Never use anything smaller than 10-point or larger than 12-point type for the body of your resume. Heads and sub-heads, of course, should be slightly larger.

6.  **Choose a face and stick with it.** Unless you're a graphic design major, resist the urge to play with typefaces. When amateurs try to do too much "designing," the results are inevitably …amateurish.

7.  **Highlight key points with boldface type**. While you shouldn't mix typefaces, you can use boldface (very dark) versions of the same typeface to emphasize and draw attention to key elements—your name, names of organizations, employers, schools, and headlines.

8.  **Use ALL CAPS and underlining sparingly, if at all**. Never underline words or phrases in your body copy. Research shows capitalizing and/or underlining whole words just slows the eye while reading. If you *must*, consider using all caps or underlining for your name and section heads only.

9.  **Avoid *italic* type.** Your goal should be to emphasize key elements of your resume through punchy writing and proper layout, so italics as a means of emphasis would be redundant, even a distraction, since italic type is harder to read.

10.  **Employ generous margins.** Leave at least an inch of white space at the top of each page and, if possible, one inch on the other three sides (but never less than ½ inch). Narrow margins "choke" a document; wide margins create a more pleasant, uncluttered look.

11.  **Use a "ragged right" layout.** Don't worry about "justifying" or "evening out" your right margin; just let each line end naturally:

This paragraph uses a ragged right style. Notice how the uneven line breaks create attractive white space around the edges. A justified paragraph looks "boxy" and places needed white space between words instead of at the end of lines.

12.  **Avoid hyphens.** They break up words and, as a result, the "flow" of a hiring manager's eye, as he or she digests your qualifications. By avoiding hyphens, you eliminate such interruptions.

13.  **Single space within listings** and double space (or more, if necessary) between sections and paragraphs. Correct spacing creates an attractive, balanced look.

14.  **Use bullets to highlight accomplishments,** but try to limit the size of bulleted items to two lines. Key points can be camouflaged in a paragraph format—bullets help you deliver a large number of selling points in a crisp, telegraph-like style. If you make your bullets too long, you've defeated their purpose and merely guaranteed that your resume will shoot blanks.

15.  **Limit your paragraphs to four or five lines.** Otherwise, again, too much information will be lost, rather than emphasized.

16.  **Shorten your line length.** The shorter the distance your eye has to travel across a page, the easier the copy is to read. I've already suggested a one-inch margin all around. Now I'm going to also suggest that you indent all body copy two more inches from the left margin, leaving only section heads and dates to the left. There are several sample resumes later in this book that effectively use this format. I think it looks exceedingly clean. It also works wonders when you want to fill an entire page with a high school diploma and two summer jobs!

17. **Keep it simple, stupid (KISS).** Once you find a design you like, stick with it. Don't over-design your resume or try to include a smattering of different styles. It will only make your resume look confused.

18. **Find your own simple format.** The sample resumes in this book come in a wide variety of styles. Find one you like, modify it if necessary...and create your own perfect resume!

## Don't go job hunting without them

While resume styles do vary, there are three essentials that absolutely can't be left out:

1.  **Your name, address, telephone number, and e-mail address.** This information should be printed at the top of your resume. If possible, include both day and evening telephone numbers, designating them "Home" and "Office" (rather than, "Home" and "Girlfriend's Place.") If your current e-mail address is silly or playful, set up an account with a more professional sound(*nsmith@mail.com* as opposed to *sweetiepie@mail.com*). A silly e-mail might be a turn-off to prospective employers.

2.  **Education and training.** This is the meat of the resume for students.

3.  **Skills and experience.** This is the most important part of the resume for anyone with job experience. Include information on your employment, relevant volunteer experiences, and other extracurricular accomplishments.

## Optional elements

### A job objective

This is a brief statement that describes the kind of job you want. It should appear at the top of the resume, directly under your name, address, phone number, and e-mail address. Many experts object to the inclusion of job objectives because they usually are as compelling as a soup label.

Those experts who do encourage applicants to include a job objective suggest a clear, concise description, such as:

*   Position as a commercial art illustrator or cartoonist.
*   Administrative assistant to corporate officer.
*   Computer programmer specializing in computer-aided engineering and computer-aided design.

Statements like these indicate that you have a good idea where you want to be in your career. They also make it easy for the person initially screening the resume to know immediately what position you're after.

But that in itself can present some problems. For instance, let's say you're interested in working for a company called Springer Motors because you've heard wonderful things about its career advancement policies and training program. You hear about an opening in the customer service department and apply for it, writing an ad hoc objective on your resume, such as, "A customer-service position offering career advancement."

Well, you might be interested in other jobs at Springer because it's known to be a wonderful place to work, but the screener at Springer certainly won't know that from your resume. In fact, she might get no further than this line of your resume before removing you from the running.

Think about that career objective from a marketing standpoint: It talks about what *you* want. Employers (your "customers") are looking for what you can offer *them*.

However, there are circumstances in which no one would argue with your decision to include a career objective on your resume. Here are two of them:

1.  **If you are interested in one specific job.** If you're sure that it is the only one that will satisfy you, then by all means state your precise objective and go for broke.

2.  **If your career goal would be difficult for employers to understand.** Let's say you are interested in switching careers or taking your current career in a slightly new direction. It makes good sense to state a clear objective. For instance, a friend of mine with 15 years of magazine publishing experience decided to move into public relations. The objective he included on his resume read:

*To use the news sense and editing abilities developed in various editorial positions to help a public relations firm meet its clients' marketing communication needs.*

## A summary of qualifications

The current rage in resumes is the qualifications summary. A summary is a resume in a nutshell, intended to capture the essence of your experience in one or two sentences. Here's an example:

*Strong background in metallurgy, including several internships with a leading engineering firm and two published articles in leading journals. Thorough knowledge of computer modeling techniques and programming.*

If you're using your resume as part of a career direct-mail package, then the summary of qualifications is usually essential. After all, it allows you to showcase areas of strong expertise for a potential employer who might miss them in scanning the body of your resume.

However, don't include a summary unless you have a lot of things to sum up. If you're fresh out of school and don't have internships or relevant experience, then save the selling copy for the body of the resume.

But, if your education has been highly focused, enabling you to document extensive and intensive coursework in an applicable area, or if you have specific (if limited) experience that perfectly matches your objective, I'd include such a section.

To illustrate, consider the case of a graduate student seeking an entry-level position in marketing research. The objective might read:

*A position in marketing, with emphasis on research, planning, and concept development, for a product-oriented company.*

The matching qualifications statement might read:

*Intensive coursework in business administration, including statistical methodology, market research, management, strategic planning and new product development, plus 25 graduate-level credits in accounting and business law. Summer internship in the Marketing Department of CBS Records.*

## Volunteer experience

Should you really include Little League coaching and your participation in charitable organizations on your resume? Absolutely. It will demonstrate that you're a good citizen and might even demonstrate leadership skills.

## Outside interests

As an employer, I've always smirked at the "personal data" sections of resumes. After all, everyone has outside interests of some kind, unless they are turnips. Do most people really think they will be successful in their job search because they told employers they were interested in "music, reading and home décor?" It's best to talk about experience that demonstrates knowledge *applicable to your chosen career* and traits, such as reliability, that all employers are looking for in applicants.

If you're trying to get a job at *Pizza Today* magazine and you've worked your way up to weekend night manager after four years of part-time work at the local parlor, obviously you have pertinent experience. Likewise, if you're trying to get a job at the local pizzeria, noting somewhere that you've subscribed to *Pizza Today* for years *would* be pertinent. But unless something you've done outside school, job, and volunteer work is *directly pertinent* to the job at hand, such personal information is just filling space.

Having said that, I could make a case for including involvement in activities that indirectly "state your case"—those you could cite to illustrate your sense of responsibility, ambition, attention to detail, ability to work with a team, etc. Just be sure you're ready to defend the pertinence of any such inclusions.

Having said *that*, you should still resist the urge to include anything that might be considered controversial. Why crow about your passion for PETA when the hiring manager could be a fur fanatic?

## Awards and honors

What better testimony to your diligence, intelligence, and/or commitment than receiving a meaningful award or honor from a recognized organization? List those awards that are most related to your job goal. Membership in Phi Beta Kappa or the National Honor Society is evidence of your educational achievements. Winning an award for community service might speak of your leadership capabilities.

## Professional and social organizations

The value of taking up valuable space to lists membership organizations, especially those to which you've merely sent dues, is negligible. If any of them are religious or political, you'll probably want to omit them for different reasons. Why invite prejudice when you don't have to? It may only get your resume trashed before you've even had a chance to show them what a sterling candidate you are! Citing your years of involvement with the Teenage Democratic Club probably won't get you an interview with the manager who has pictures of *both* Presidents Bush over his desk.

On the other hand, what if you have little or no job history but a lot of experience with your church, synagogue, or other religious or service group? You have no choice—include what you achieved and outline your responsibilities for each position. And if you are a recent high school or college graduate, activities that show you're a well-rounded individual with the ability to manage a busy schedule are probably pertinent. Unless they're directly related to the job at hand, keep any such entries very brief—the name of the organization and any leadership positions you hold (or held).

## Military experience

The longer you were in the military—and the more pertinent your training to the job you're seeking—the more room your experience deserves on the resume. The technical skills you acquired may be particularly important, but so are *any* accomplishments that will help your resume stand out. Many employers believe the military develops character, leadership, and team-building skills. Shouldn't you take advantage of their bias in your favor?

This is especially true if your only experience *is* in the military. Since it's been your only "job", you need to give it the weight it deserves.

If the work you're seeking has little or nothing to do with the particular duties and responsibilities you developed in the service, you may choose to  list only the highest rank you achieved and where you were stationed.

# There are some definite *no*'s

Various experts may argue the pros and cons of including some of the items just discussed. But I doubt many of them would do anything but shudder at the thought of including the following:

1. **Photographs or illustrations (of yourself or anything else).** Unless required by your profession (acting, modeling), there's no reason to include to include photos of any kind, or even elements of a physical description (height, weight, etc.).

2. **The reason you left past jobs.** You certainly know by now that including *any* negative information on a resume is grounds for immediate spanking. But even if you left a job for *positive* reasons—a promotion, a transfer, you were spirited away by the competition—such details do not belong on your resume. Wait for the question to come up in the interview, as it invariably will, and make sure you have rehearsed a truthful and concise reply.

3. **References.** While you should prepare a separate sheet containing the names and contact information of your references, it should not be included in the resume itself. Nor do you need to add "References available upon request" or some such phrase at the bottom of your resume, since most employers would assume they are.

4. **Salary information,** either past salaries or your present requirement. Since it's doubtful you've made enough to have your past salary be much of an issue, the real key is avoiding the subject of the salary you *want*. Why do so many employers request such information in their ads and Web-postings? Because they want to see how cheaply they can get you! There is no reason to make their job easier—if you must supply a target salary, make it a range and include it in your cover letter, *not* on your resume.

5. **Feelings about travel or relocation.** If they're *positive*, include them in a cover letter, especially if either is a job requirement. If you *don't* want to travel, and are absolutely dead set against relocating, why would you even *think* of including that on your resume? Then again, why would you be applying for a job that requires either?

6. **Testimonials.** So you, "Produced an ad during an internship that the creative director said was the best he'd ever seen." Do you really believe that, "Editor-in-chief of school newspaper said I was the next Woodward (or Bernstein)" is going to get you a job? These unsupported testimonials will do you

absolutely no good whatsoever and do not belong on your resume (or even in your cover letter, *unless* you *actually have* a letter from the pertinent person that substantiates your claim to fame).

7. **Personal statistics.** In our litigious age, employers are more wary than ever of claims that they discriminated against potential job candidates. So, they do not really welcome details about your looks, age, marital status, and health. Better to fill the space on your resume with information about your *job* qualifications, not facts about your personal life that *should* be irrelevant to today's employer.

8. **Personality profiles.** While describing yourself as "enthusiastic," "highly motivated," and an "excellent self-starter" will not send a worried employer to his or her legal department for advice, it won't do you much good, either. Since employers don't exactly expect candidates to own up to their character flaws on the resume, they give little or no weight to such self-aggrandizing phrases.

9. **The word "Resume" at the top of the page.** Is there an employer out there who *doesn't* recognize a resume when he or she sees one? Not likely. No need for a title. Save the line, and add one more scintillating detail to your self-portrait.

## Use power words for impact

Be brief. Use phrases rather than complete sentences. Choose your words carefully, and use "power words" whenever possible. "Organized" is more powerful than "put together"; "supervised," better than "oversaw"; and "formulated," better than "thought up." Strong words like these can make the most mundane internship or part-time position sound like Ted Turner's job. (Just kidding. I'm not encouraging you to exaggerate.) Here's a starter list of words that you may want to use in your resume:

| | | |
|---|---|---|
| achieved | implemented | managed |
| administered | improved | negotiated |
| advised | initiated | operated |
| analyzed | instituted | organized |
| applied | instructed | overhauled |
| arranged | introduced | planned |
| budgeted | invented | prepared |
| calculated | issued | presented |
| classified | launched | presided |
| communicated | lectured | programmed |

| | | |
|---|---|---|
| completed | litigated | promoted |
| computed | lobbied | recommended |
| coordinated | managed | researched |
| critiqued | negotiated | reviewed |
| delegated | implemented | revised |
| determined | improved | reorganized |
| developed | initiated | regulated |
| devised | instituted | selected |
| directed | instructed | solved |
| established | introduced | scheduled |
| evaluated | invented | supervised |
| executed | issued | tested |
| formulated | launched | traced |
| gathered | lectured | trained |
| generated | litigated | updated |
| guided | lobbied | utilized |

To be on the safe side, I would suggest including both "power" verbs and key words on your resume.

## A word about the electronic resume

There is one more type of resume every job hunter should be familiar with—the electronic resume. More large- and medium-sized companies— as many as 78 percent according to one study—are having computers scan and sort the thousands of resumes they receive according to "key words." In general, the more key words the computer detects, the better your chances of making the first cut—which will lead to the first "human screening."

Just what is a "key word"? It may be a company name, a number of years of experience, or a degree. Many key words identify very specific terminology that defines the requisites of a particular job at a particular company. For example, the key words for a device analysis engineer might include "device physics," "failure analysis," "bipolar technologies," and "BS (degree)."

How will you know if your resume will be scanned (as opposed to being hand-sorted by a real human being)? You probably won't. As a result, many career consultants are recommending that job hunters load up on key words—beginning with those that appear in the company's posted advertisements.

Whether *chronological* or *functional* in format, electronic resumes tend to alter some of the advice that I've already given you. For example, did you notice that not a single one of the sample key words I listed was a verb? The computer software that scans resumes tends to search for nouns—job titles, for instance—better than verbs. Here are more changes to keep in mind:

- **Computers don't read cover letters.** Your electronic resume has to do the selling job of both.
- **It's okay to go to two pages, even three.** All the more room for key words. However, I wouldn't recommend sending volumes. Your resume will ultimately be reviewed by a human who is likely to have fairly traditional ideas about resumes.
- **Computers are easily confused by boldface, underlined and italic type.** A computer scanner also may not be able to recognize an unusual font. (For a resume that will be scanned, a sans serif font is better than the serif fonts recommended for "paper" resumes.)
- **Design a key-word resume solely for use online and via e-mail.** That way you can re-design it completely, emphasizing key words, eliminating boldface and italics, using a different font, etc.

## Posting your resume online

It's impossible to include a detailed discussion of electronic resumes in this short book. It's also unnecessary since there is a wonderful book available that will tell you absolutely everything you need to know—the brand-new second edition of Rebecca Smith's *Electronic Resumes and Online Networking* (Career Press, 2000). With her permission, I have included a very brief introduction to this topic below. I urge you to read her book if you are also planning to prepare an electronic resume, as I suspect most of you are:

Chances are, you will post your resume for computer audiences in one of three ways. You will send it via e-mail, send it via an electronic form (e-form), or create a Web page.

Posting your resume on the Internet is analogous to posting a "Ben Hogan golf clubs for sale" flier on a bulletin board where the public can see it. A resume posted on the Internet is usually stored in a database, where thousands of employers and recruiters can retrieve it and view your qualifications. How do you decide which job posting service to use? Test several. Results vary by software and technology used.

With the three posting methods, you'd think all you have to do it create a resume and randomly post it on many Web sites. But random resume posting will probably produce the same results as mass-mailed resumes—nothing. Targeting the right audiences for making your skills known will affect how your resume is retrieved when recruiters and employers are searching. The challenge in posting is that you never really know who will view your resume, and in what condition it will arrive...if at all. All you know is whether it generated any interviews. To overcome this problem, pay attention to preparing your resume based on the method you choose for posting it in a way that maximizes your chances of getting noticed. There are certain "controls" you can implement to monitor the success of your resume once it has been posted.

In all cases, where you decide to post your resume will determine how you will prepare it.

## Just fill in the blanks

At the end of this chapter, I've prepared a fill-in-the-blanks resume form that will allow you to create a good rough draft of a resume within minutes. List everything you've done, even if it seems trivial. There's a potential job out there for which that "trivial" skill or experience may be the key!

## Fill-in-the-blanks resume outline

Name _____

Address _____

City, state, zip _____

Telephone number _____

E-mail address _____

Objective _____

_____

Summary of qualifications _____

_____

_____

_____

_____

_____

# Education

Graduate school _____

City, state _____

Graduation date (expected) _____

Degree earned (expected) _____

Grade point average _____Class rank _____

Important classes you have taken, especially those that relate to your expected career _____

_____

_____

_____

_____

_____

College _____

City, state _____

Graduation date (expected) _____

Degree earned (expected) _____

Grade point average _____Class rank _____

Major _____ Minor _____

Important classes you have taken, especially those that relate to your expected career _____

_____

_____

_____

_____

High school _____

City, state _____

Graduation date (expected) _____

Grade point average _____ Class rank _____

Important classes you have taken, especially those that relate to your expected career _____

_____

_____

_____

## Hobbies and other interests (optional)

_____

_____

_____

**Extracurricular activities** (Activity name, dates participated, duties and responsibilities, offices held, accomplishments) _____

_____

_____

_____

_____

_____

_____

_____

_____

**Awards and honors** (Award name, from who and date received, significance of the award, and any other pertinent details) _____

_____

_____

_____

_____

_____

_____

_____

_____

_____

**Work experience** (Include job title, name of business, address, phone number, dates of employment, supervisor's name and title, your major responsibilities, accomplishments, and any awards won. Include volunteer experience in this category. List your experiences with the most recent dates first, even if you later decide not to use a chronological format.)

_____

_____

_____

_____

_____

_____

_____

_____

**References** (Though you should not include references in your resume, you do need to prepare a separate list of at least three people who know you fairly well and will recommend you highly to prospective employers. For each, include job title, company name, address, and telephone number. Before you include anyone on this list, make sure you have permission to use his or her name as a reference, and confirm what he or she intends to say about you to a potential employer.)

1. _____

_____

_____

2. _____

_____

_____

3. _____

_____

_____

4. _____

_____

_____

5. _____

_____

_____

# Chapter 9

# Editing and Rewriting Your Resume

Ernest Hemingway once explained, "I write standing up and edit sitting down." Meaning that getting that first draft down is the easy part—you could do it standing up—but the editing was where the real work was done.

If you've gathered and organized all the information for your resume, maybe even used the fill-in-the-blanks form I just provided, you have just written your rough draft. How do you make it better? How do you make it *sing?* Start by looking at the big changes you have to make. Make them. Then look at each detail and see how it can be improved or corrected. Here are some questions to ask to make these jobs easier.

## The "big" questions

### Have I chosen the right format?

Does the resume format I've chosen highlight my pluses? Does it suggest there are skeletons hiding in the closet?

### Have I communicated to the employer that I can fill a need?

Does it tell the employer what I can do for her...right now? Will it make her confident that I am qualified and motivated, confident enough to give me a chance? Would it convince *me* to give this inexperienced kid a chance?

### Have I emphasized my strengths and eliminated weaknesses?

There may be problems you have to solve, weaknesses you have to reveal, decisions and choices you have to defend—in your cover letter or in the interview—but they do *not* belong on your resume. Highlight your strengths and make sure how you've phrased or formatted specific information doesn't automatically raise questions you don't really want to answer just yet.

### Is my resume too long or cluttered?

Is it longer than two pages or, if not, does it appear jam-packed? If so, what can I remove? Does my list of volunteer activities relate to the job at hand? Does it identify qualities this employer will value? What does my list of hobbies say about me? What's redundant? What's unnecessary?

*Does every element count?*

Is the job objective meaningful and targeted, or does it sound as exciting as the prose in my accounting textbook? Did I put my best foot forward in the skills summary? Are all those memberships I listed going to mean squat to this employer? Are all of the elements crisp and exciting? If not, eliminate or "punch" them up. Don't waste valuable space on anything that doesn't communicate your value and accomplishments.

## Put your resume under the microscope

Once you have answered the big questions and changed your resume accordingly, it's time to examine every line, every detail, to make sure it's Army-solid—"the best it can be." Here's a checklist of more questions to help you through this detailed editing process:

*Name header*

- Are my name, address, phone number, and e-mail address clearly displayed at the top of the page?
- Did I use the most professional-sounding version of my name (Frances instead of Cookie, William rather than Billy Bob)?
- Did I include my correct address? If I'm moving, did I indicate my future address and the date I'll be there?
- Did I include a phone number at which I can be easily (and reliably) reached or at which messages can be left? Did I include my area code? Check that numbers have not been transposed—it's an all-too-common mistake.

*Job objective*

- Have I stated it in 12 or fewer words?
- Is it focused and precise, stating exactly the position I want?
- Does it mesh with the rest of my resume? Is it supported by my education, skills and experience?
- Does it preclude my being considered for other positions at the same company? If so, should I draft alternate versions of my resume that feature different objectives?

*Skills summary*

- Is it targeted to the job I'm seeking?
- Does it highlight the qualifications and experience most pertinent to *this* prospective employer?
- Is it short and concise—two or three brief sentences, four or five bulleted points?
- Have I placed my most relevant qualification first?

## Experience profile

In chronological resumes

- Did I include the correct starting and ending dates (month and year) for each job, internship, and volunteer activity?
- Did I use the correct job title for each? If I "revised" it to sound a bit more important, did I choose a title that might mislead or be considered deceitful?
- Did I include the correct names of all employers and organizations? The correct locations?
- Did I use short, punchy sentences to describe each job?
- Are any of the paragraphs used to describe any jobs or activities longer than five lines?

In functional and combination resumes

- Are the skill categories I chose the most relevant to the job I want?
- Did I use business-oriented terms (e.g., "Childcare" rather than "Baby sitting")?
- Did I include a brief chronological listing of paid/volunteer experience near the end of the resume?

In all resume formats

- Did I use strong action words to describe contributions and achievements?
- Have I *over*used particular words?
- Did I eliminate unnecessary articles such as "I", "the" and "an"?
- Did I use acronyms, abbreviations or terms that might not be understood by everyone reading my resume?
- Did I *quantify* accomplishments rather than simply describe them? Did I talk about the amount of money saved or by what percentage I increased sales, decreased expenses, increased participation, saved time, etc.?
- Did I use the correct name for each honor or award received? Did I correctly identify the organization that gave it and the year it was received? Did I highlight *why* I received it?

## Education

- Did I check the dates I attended each school and when I received degrees?
- Did I identify each degree correctly?
- Did I check the name and location of each school?
- Did I correctly list the dates I received certifications or licenses?

*Miscellaneous*

- If I listed memberships in various organizations, did I check the correct name and spelling of each one?
- Did I include any of the items Ron previously suggested I omit— the word "resume," salary history, etc.? Eliminate them!

*Style*

- Did I leave a generous margin all around (at least one inch at the top and one-half inch all around)?
- Did I use a serif typeface?
- Is the type large enough to be easily read (no less than 10 pt.)?
- Did I leave the right margin ragged?
- Did I use underlining and ALL CAPS sparingly, if at all?
- Did I use boldface type sparingly but wisely? Are the words I emphasized in this way the ones I want an employer to notice first?
- Did I use spacing to break up large blocks of information?
- If my resume is longer than a page, did I write "continued" on the bottom of page one and my name and "page 2 of 2" at the top of the second page?
- Did I use some kind of bullets or asterisks to emphasize specific points in the listings?
- Is my style consistent throughout? Did I use the same type, type size, and format for heads, subheads, listings, etc.?

## Recheck speling and, grammar

One typo can easily send your resume on the fast track to the trash bin. Why lose a great opportunity just because you transposed a letter or misspelled a name? Now is the time to make sure your resume is absolutely perfect. Here are some proofreading tricks to help you achieve that:

- **Get out a ruler and go through your resume one line at a time.** This will force you to slow down your reading and focus on each word.
- **Don't rely solely on your computer's spell-check program.** Some of them still don't recognize the difference between "there" and "their" or that you wrote "you" when you meant "your". Check it the old-fashioned way—word by word, line by line.
- **Read from the bottom up...and backwards.** This will, again, force you to read much more slowly. Since you won't be able to make any sense of sentences, you won't be able to focus on anything but the words themselves.

+ **Get some help from family and friends.** You've probably learned from a term paper or two that the "closer" you are to the writing, the harder it seems to be to spot even obvious errors. Have someone with "fresh eyes" give your resume a careful read.

+ **Read it aloud.** This will not check the words themselves but rather how each *line* reads. It will help you eliminate unnecessary words and ensure you haven't omitted a key word!

After you've proofread once, proof it again. And a third time. Remember: Many, if not most, employers *will* simply throw away a resume that contains *any* errors. Once you're convinced it is perfect, you're ready to create the final product.

## Printing your masterpiece

The printing choices you need to make now must meet the same objectives you had when designing your resume in the first place: You want it to be neat, clean, and easy to read. What you *don't* want to do is detract from the excellent design choices you made by making poor or inconsistent printing choices.

If you created your resume on a computer or word processor, you should have no problem printing out a master original on a laser printer or good quality ink-jet printer. If you do not have a computer or access to one, you can have your local copy or "quick print" shop professionally typeset your resume. Since this is a relatively expensive option, make it a priority to find (or make!) a friend with a computer and printer.

Once you have a clean original—on the whitest, brightest paper you can find—the local "quick print" shop is your only printing option. Do not mimeograph it, photocopy it, or simply create copies by retyping it with carbons. None will give you the look you want. You will inevitably end up with a resume that has smudges, streaks, or inconsistent ink coverage, all to save a few cents.

The only choice left to make now is paper stock:

**Select a white, off-white, ivory, or buff-colored paper.** These ensure readability and professionalism, unlike pink, bright blue, or some other garish background color.

**Choose a good quality, medium-weight paper.** Good quality copy paper is 50#. Select a 60# or even a 70# paper with high opacity.

**Avoid glossy or textured stock.** Your resume isn't a magazine, so avoid glossy magazine stock. A simple textured background is allowed, as long as it doesn't hinder readability.

**Buy matching envelopes and stationery.** And, naturally, print your return address on the envelope and a nice heading on the stationery using a typeface compatible with your resume. Don't "overdesign" your stationery or include pictures or illustrations on it.

**Stick with black or, at worst, a deep blue or brown ink.** This is not the time to see how hot pink ink will look on a mauve background.

I have received, believe it or not, scarred, beaten-up, even stained resumes over the years. What were those applicants thinking? Please take the few minutes necessary to ensure the package you send out to a potential boss doesn't label you a slob...who is *not* going to be interviewed, thank you.

Your resume should be kept up-to-date but never by penciling in a note or change, no matter how neatly. *If you have to make a change, produce a new master and make new copies.* The resume you send out must *always* be perfect, flawless, pristine, virgin, untouched. Have I over-emphasized this point enough?

---

## Vicki Bacal's 10 Steps to a Winning Resume

1. Address the reader's needs, answering the question, "Why should I hire you?"
2. Highlight outstanding characteristics in a rapid-fire Summary of Qualifications to provide a quick overview.
3. Tell the reader how you made a difference.
4. Be clear, concise, and specific. Use facts and figures to add credibility.
5. Emphasize your key accomplishments with short sentences and descriptive verbs to gain and hold the reader's attention.
6. Use repetition of key ideas to remind the reader of your greatest strengths and achievements.
7. Let the reader know that you understand the industry by using insider terminology.
8. Use attractive graphics, white space, underlining, and boldface to draw reader interest.
9. Highlight on-the-job and continuing education to emphasize current knowledge and augment undergraduate education.
10. Take credit for your role in successful projects. Cite examples of leadership, initiative, and accomplishment.

---

Vicki Bacal, president of The Resume Specialist in Minneapolis, MN, has advised more than 10,000 clients nationwide since 1985 in the areas of resume writing, interview preparation, and job search strategy.

Excerpted from *Resumes, Resumes, Resumes,* Copyright 1997 The Career Press.

# Chapter 10

# A Variety of Sample Resumes

I know, I know. You're still not sure how your resume should look, whether you should include the "bells and whistles"—career objectives, the summary of qualifications, or the personal data sections we talked about in Chapter 8.

This chapter contains 37 sample resumes, covering a broad array of professions and experience levels. I have sprinkled various styles and formats throughout so that you can really do some "window shopping" before deciding how you want to present yourself to prospective employers.

The purpose of this chapter is to give you concrete examples of how other people in similar circumstances have styled their resumes. Despite their differences, all of the samples included have a number of ingredients in common, the same ingredients your resume must contain. Each is:

- Cleanly and clearly typed or typeset.
- Logically and simply organized.
- Simply laid out, with as much white space as the information will allow.
- Short and concise.
- Targeted to the prospective employer.
- Designed to emphasize strengths and de-emphasize weaknesses.
- In the format that is most appropriate to the education, experience, and skills of each person.

## Try before you buy

The following guide will help you locate those resumes most pertinent to your own situation:

## Samples of formats

## Resumes for high school graduates applying for employment

## Resumes for high school graduates applying to post-secondary institutions

## Resumes for college graduates: liberal arts majors

## Resumes for college graduates: engineering/science majors

## Resumes for other "first timers"

## Resumes for short-term employment

As you'll see, I have sprinkled various formats, styles, and typefaces throughout, so whatever your situation, you should look over all the samples.

What if a sample resume for the particular job you're looking for isn't included? The odds, are it won't be. But it shouldn't be hard to adapt one of the samples to your particular situation, since they cover, in general, all the possibilities. In most cases, merely tailoring the objective to your own circumstances and replacing information in the other sections with your own educational and work experience would result in a superior resume.

## A matter of style

The style and format you will use in your own resume is really more a question of emphasis than anything else. The chronological and functional resume formats can be used almost interchangeably, though for most students, the chronological is preferred.

Unless you have a long list of skills, it's preferable to highlight your educational background. But if your skills inventory is exceptionally broad, you will want to highlight it—even if your work experience is very limited. In this circumstance, the functional format would probably work best. The combination format is best used when you have considerable work experience.

The traditional sequencing for the three types of resume formats follows:

| **Chronological:** | **Functional:** | **Combination:** |
|---|---|---|
| Contact information | Contact information | Contact information |
| Objective | Objective | Objective |
| Qualifications | Qualifications | Qualifications |
| Education | Skills/achievements | Skills/achievements |
| Work experience | Education | Work experience |
| | | Education |

## Chronological resume

Michelle Lee ◆ 21 College Ave. ◆ Lafayette, IN 46099 ◆ (317) 555-6126

**Objective**

Position as a veterinarian with a small animal practice, with emphasis in feline medicine and surgery.

**Summary of Qualifications**

Excellent training and experience in small animal surgery and treatment. Good background in office management and inventory control. Well-developed client relations skills.

**Education**

DVM, Purdue University School of Veterinary Medicine West Lafayette, IN (5.7/6.0 GPA) Expected graduation, May 2000.

**Significant clerkship and course work**: Clinical Pathology, Opthamology/ Small Animal Medicine, Small Animal Surgery, Client Relations, Non-Domestic Animal Medicine

**Work Experience**

**Lakeside Animal Hospital, Sturgis, MI** (July-September 1999 internship)

- ◆ Performed and assisted with small and large animal surgery.
- ◆ Managed office and medical supplies inventory.
- ◆ Assisted on farm calls and handled seven after-hours emergencies.
- ◆ Recommended and implemented new computer software, which enhanced customer service and patient care.

**Animal Disease Diagnostic Lab, Purdue University** (September 1997-May 1999)

- ◆ Performed necropsies on a variety of species.

**Sturgis Veterinary Clinic, Sturgis, MI** (Summers 1997, 1998)

- ◆ Completed small animal surgery, treatments, and radiography.
- ◆ Performed clinical lab work and assisted on farm calls.
- ◆ Learned to work with clients, answer questions, and address concerns.
- ◆ Supervised transition from manual to computerized record keeping, resulting in more accurate patient records and an enhanced check-up reminder program.

**Lab Technician, Purdue University** (January-August 1996)

- ◆ Prepared and interpreted histopathology slides.
- ◆ Collected bovine blood samples.
- ◆ Ran reproductive hormone assays.
- ◆ Implemented new report procedure, providing clients with more detailed information.

## Functional resume

Christopher Morrow
55 Center Drive ◆ Coatsville, FL ◆ 32310 ◆ (305) 555-9745
morrow@mailbox.com

### Skills/Abilities

Organizational/Management
- Handled stocking and assisted in managing flow of stock in grocery store
- Prepared weekly inventory reports and submitted to supervisor
- Recommended new stocking system, which reduced stocking time by four hours a week
- Served as treasurer of high school RC airplane club for two years
- Coordinated candy sale fund raiser for RC airplane club, which resulted in $350 in profit
- Helped plan monthly "flyings" and quarterly meetings

Customer Relations
- Assisted grocery shoppers in finding products
- Provided carry out service
- Created new customer comment program, which included a personal letter from the appropriate department head and increased customer satisfaction by 75%
- Served 78 customers on neighborhood newspaper route and handled billing and collections
- Initiated revised billing program for paper route, which increased on-time payments by 30%

Communication
- Wrote articles about RC airplane club for high school newspaper

### Work History

Stock clerk, Superthrift, Maddington, FL (Summers and after school, June 1998-current)
Newspaper carrier, *Daily Times,* Coatsville, FL (June 1996-June 1998)

### Education

Graduate, Washington High School, Coatsville, FL (June 2000)

## Combination resume

### Laurie Kelly
1523 15th Street, Apt. A8
Washington, DC  20005
202-555-1212
LKelly@Simpro.net

**OBJECTIVE:** A professional sales position in information processing where administrative and technical experience, initiative, and interpersonal skills can be used to maximize sales.

### SALES/CUSTOMER RELATIONS:

- Worked in sales support as liaison between technical staff and end-users.

- Demonstrated ability to find solutions to customer problems and work to create user-friendly systems.

### PLANNING/ORGANIZING:

- Planned and reorganized sales support system.

- Initiated cost accounting studies that saved the company $45,000 in annual labor costs and improved personnel efficiency and morale.

- Developed technical reference library and database for more effective use of equipment and faster access to customer information.

### TECHNICAL:

- Two years of experience in programming IBM mainframe computers.

- Two years of experience working in a networked workstation environment.

### EXPERIENCE:

- MCT Corporation, Washington, DC, 1999-present.

- Sears Roebuck & Co., Washington, DC, 1997-1999.

### EDUCATION:

B.A. in Communication, George Mason University, Fairfax, VA, 2001.

- Courses in interpersonal communication, psychology, and public speaking.

- Worked full-time, earning 100% of educational and personal expenses.

## Cashier

Jenna LaRocco
47 London Way
Acworth, GA 30101
404-555-8234
Jenlar@alo.com

**OBJECTIVE**     A full-time cashier position in a large retail store, preferably in a shopping center in Acworth vicinity.

**EXPERIENCE**

1999-2000
(part-time)

**Cashier**, Kroger Supermarket
Acworth, GA.
Worked 20 hours a week as cashier at checkout counter.

1999-2000
(summers)

**Assistant Bookkeeper and Cashier,**
Howard's Retail Store, Acworth, GA.
Collected and recorded mail-order payments as well as those made in person at credit office; prepared monthly statements; helped bookkeeper in all record keeping.

1997-1999
(part-time)

**Accounts Receivable Clerk,**
Homowak Mart, Marietta, GA.
Received payments made in credit office and by mail, recorded cash, issued receipts; prepared monthly statements to customers.

**EDUCATION**

2000

Completed six-month course in Business Machines at Bartow Business School.

1997-2000

Attended Green Dell High School.

Completed requirements for Commercial Diploma.

# Secretary

**Melissa Kennedy**
533 Syracuse Lane
Bloomington, MN 55437
612-555-6623
Mely14@nis.net

## CAREER GOAL

A secretarial or administrative assistant position.

## SUMMARY OF SKILLS

### Organizational

- Created responsibilities manual for volunteers at county hospital, which reduced overlapping duties and increased efficiency.
- Assisted in managing volunteers for outpatient information desk at hospital.

### Secretarial

- Experienced in document formatting, proofreading and administrative assistant duties.
- Skilled in Microsoft Word and Excel on IBM compatible system.
- Ability to type 70 words per minute with no errors.

### Communication

- Delivered a speech to local civic clubs on the importance of hospital volunteers, which brought in seven new volunteers.
- Wrote articles for local newspaper on vocational team's achievements at district and state contests.

## EDUCATION

### Bloomington High School, Bloomington, MN

(Current GPA is 3.7/4.0) Graduation expected June 2002

## RELATED COURSE WORK

Bookkeeping I & II, Advanced Typing, Computer Operations, Word Processing I & II, Business Writing, Vocational Business Curriculum (2 years)

## AWARDS

Outstanding Volunteer, County Hospital (1999)

## MEMBERSHIPS

- Business Professional of America (student member)
- Minnesota Association of Hospital Volunteers
- Jr. Rotarian

# Four-year college

Kaitlin Harris
80 Outer Freeway
Dallas, TX 75260
806-555-0782
Kaitlin74@user.net

**OBJECTIVE**

Acceptance to a Midwest liberal arts college with a superior program in English literature.

**EDUCATION**

Graduating in June 2002, from Dethis High School (Dallas, TX).
College prep core curriculum including honors English 11 and 12.
GPA 3.2 (A = 4.0)

**ACTIVITIES**

Writers Club (president—1999-2000); Yearbook staff (editor—2000-2001); Field hockey (4 years); Cheer squad (3 years); United Way.

**HONORS & AWARDS**

National Honor Society, Senior Class President.

**EXPERIENCE**

**Kiach Publishing Co.** (Dallas, TX)
2000 & 2001 (summers)
Editorial intern.
Duties included reading manuscripts, typing editors' reports, filing.

**Simmons Public Library** (Simmons, TX)
2000 & 2001 (school year)
Library assistant.
Duties included cataloging, typing, and filing.

## Four-year college

**BRIAN EPSTEIN**
**221 Boylston Street**
**Laurel, MD 20708**
**301-555-8585**

**OBJECTIVE:**

Matriculation at a Liberal Arts college to pursue study in computer science.

**EDUCATION:**

June 2002 graduate, Laurel H.S., Laurel, MD
Academic degree GPA 3.4

**ACTIVITIES:**

Math Club (Secretary), Varsity Football,
Community Relations Board, Member of Student Council

**AWARDS:**

Math Club Sigma Cup (Honors)

**EXPERIENCE:**
**Counterperson**
Big Lobster drive-in,
Cabrini Boulevard, Laurel, MD, 1999-2001 (summers)
**Stock room clerk**
R.H. Macy & Co.,
Laurel, MD, Christmas, 1999-2000

**PERSONAL:**

Red Cross Life Savers accredited.

## Two-year college

Julie Kimball
400 West Broadway
New City, NY 10956
914-555-2398
JKHome@user.net

### OBJECTIVE

Acceptance at a junior college offering a
business accounting major.

### EDUCATION

June 2001 commercial graduate, Clarkstown H.S., Nyack, NY
GPA: 3.2

### ACTIVITIES

Student government, typing pool, girls' soccer, ski teams,
and pep squad.

### AWARDS

Girls' Varsity Soccer MVP, 2001

### WORK EXPERIENCE

Clerk/typist, Alvira Insurance, Main Street, Nanuet, NY
part-time, 2000-2001

### INTERESTS

All outdoor sports, especially cross-country skiing.Fund-raising
activities for Salvation Army.

### SKILLS

Typing: 60 wpm. Shorthand: 75 wpm.

## Trade school

**John O'Sullivan**
101 St. Mark's Place
Naperville, IL 60540
708-555-0091
JJOS@mail.net

**OBJECTIVE:**      Acceptance at a trade school offering certification in electronics and TV repair.

**EDUCATION:**      June 2001 Graduate, Naperville High School, Naperville, IL. Class rank 220/490. Commercial course.

**ACTIVITIES:**      Arts & Crafts Council (president); TV Studio Club (manager).

**AWARDS:**      H.S. Emmys, Chief Stagehand/Electrician. Gold Prize, set design, 1999.

**EXPERIENCE:**      Rockland Auto Radio, Assistant Mechanic; summers 1999-2001, after school (20 hours/week).

**PERSONAL:**      Build model airplanes and small, electronically operated sailing boats.

## Photographic/Graphic Design Assistant

**Sam Jones**
123 Amber Street
Jefferson City, Missouri, 65107
sam_jones@yehaa.com

| | |
|---|---|
| EDUCATION | B.A. French Language & Literature<br>Photography<br>University of Missouri, May 2000<br>University of Paris, Sorbonne  1998-99 |
| SKILLS | Desktop Publishing—QuarkXPress<br>and Pagemaker<br>Photography—B&W and Color<br>darkroom knowledge |

SELECTED WORK
EXPERIENCE

| | |
|---|---|
| 10/00-Present | ABC Magazine—Production Intern<br>Trafficking ads through various stages<br>Clerical assistant to V.P., Production<br>Work with Destop Publishing System |
| 9/99-5/00 | University of Missouri, School of Art<br>Aiding students with use of software<br>for graphic design class |

AWARDS & PUBLICATIONS

Finalist, 1999 Photgraphy Award
Tom Jay Award, 1998, for
Photography

LANGUAGES            French, Italian

## Accountant

HARRY SHARPE
11541 North Stebbens Avenue
Amherst, MA 01002
413-555-5867

**OBJECTIVE:**          Junior accountant position in a public accounting firm.

**EDUCATION:**          Bachelor of Science, University of Massachusetts
Amherst, MA, 2001
Major: Accounting (CPA emphasis)
Minor: Computer Science
GPA: 3.62/4.00

Representative accounting courses included:

- Current Issues in Financial Accounting
- Computer-based Information Systems
- Advanced Tax Law

Representative computer science courses included:

- Computer Simulation and Modeling
- Data Processing Systems
- Database Management Systems

**RELATED EXPERIENCE:**

**Business manager,** *University Monitor,*
undergraduate newspaper (1999-2001)

- Class treasurer for all four years of college.
- Professional accounting participation, included three years in Accounting Club (two years as treasurer).

**WORK EXPERIENCE:**

**Assistant Manager**, Lucky Stores, Amherst, MA (1999-2001)

- Responsible for all facets of produce management, including inventory control, quality assurance, scheduling of hours, and supervision of personnel.

## Dietician

# Karen Burns

**2109 Park Avenue**
**Taylor Mill, KY 41015**
**606-555-0280**
**kburns@dream.net**

**JOB OBJECTIVE:**

Staff specialist position with food processing company.

**EDUCATION:**

Nutrition Major, B.S. degree, Michigan State University, 1999.

> Graduate courses on:
> - Environmental Effect on Man and His Menu
> - Special Food for the Elderly
> - Food Chemistry

These courses provided an excellent background in elements of nutrition as related to ecology, problems of the elderly, and commercial food processing.

**HONORS:**

Dean's List throughout four years of college.

**EXPERIENCE:**

Summers/1996-1999: Purdey State Hospital, Cincinnati, OH.

> **Assistant to Chief Dietitian**: Helped translate convalescent diets into actual meals; selected and delivered special meals to diet patients.

School year/1996-1997: Michigan State Student Cafeteria

> **Assistant Nutritionist**: Worked with Chief Nutritionist and her staff of 18 to plan more than 300 menus per year. Responsible for scheduling waiters and all temporary help.

**Draftsperson**

## Charles Reid
3522 Alhameda Blvd., #10
Tucson, AZ 85726
(602) 555-9162

## OBJECTIVE

A position utilizing my drafting, graphics, and computer capabilities.

## SKILLS

- Complete computer literacy; experienced in a variety of spreadsheet and word processing programs.

- Two years of precision drafting in mechanical drawing.

- Office management: filing, reception, and document authorization.

- Ability to create structured information letters for special-purpose business communications.

- Graphic arts skills applicable to offset press operations.

## EDUCATION

Currently attending Mesa Community College, Mesa, AZ.
Major courses in area of concentration: Business Communications, Word/Information Processing, Mechanical Drafting, and Electronic Drafting.

## WORK EXPERIENCE

Machinist Aide, Arrow Swiss, Phoenix, AZ (summer, 1999)
Worked under direction of owner, manufacturing small parts
requiring precision drill press and lathe operations.

## SPECIAL INTERESTS

Computers—familiar with IBM/PC and Power Macintosh.

## Housekeeper/dietician

Karen Preggers
101 South 12th Street
Philadelphia, PA 19104
(215) 555-1397

**OBJECTIVE:**   Position requiring supervisory ability as housekeeper/dietician in resort hotel or motel.

**EDUCATION:**   B.S. Cornell University, Ithaca, NY, 2000
Major: Home Economics
Minor: English
Class rank 189/854

**ACTIVITIES:**   Home Economics Club, 1997-1999
   (President, 1998-1999)
Nutrition Society of America (Chairperson, New York
   Region, 1999 and 2000)

**EXPERIENCE:**   Assistant Dietician, Henry Hudson Hotel,
Port Jervis, NY

Planned menus, functioned as hostess, and supervised
five waiters and four busboys.

## Sports reporter

Elaine Kraft
1635 Oswald Drive
Newport, RI  12840
401-555-4987

### CAREER GOAL

A position as a sports reporter or city reporter for a daily metropolitan newspaper.

### EDUCATION

May 2001

**B.A in Communications, PurdueUniversity, West Lafayette, IN**

- Graduated *With Distinction* (5.8/6.0).

- Earned minors in English and History.

- Completed career-related courses in reporting, editing, ethics in journalism, communicative law, newspaper layout and design, photography, radio and television, and magazine article writing.

### SUMMARY OF QUALIFICATIONS

- Experienced sports writer and editor.

- Strong background in newspaper mechanics, layout and design.

- Skilled in developing and implementing a variety of programs.

- Well-developed organizational and leadership skills.

- Familiarity with city government and how it operates.

### PROFESSIONAL EXPERIENCE

**Staff, *The Exponent*, Purdue University,West Lafayette, IN**

- Served as copy editor, assistant city desk editor, and assistant sports editor for campus newspaper.

- Assigned and covered city stories and sporting events.

- Established "stringer" system among nonrevenue sports, which resulted in increased coverage of those sports in the newspaper.

### CAMPUS ACTIVITIES

**Purdue University All-American Marching Band**

- Served as flag corps co-captain for two years.

- Wrote at least three new routines for the 40-member flag corps each week and scheduled extra practices when necessary.

Kraft
page 2

**Alpha Gamma Delta International Sorority**

- Completed terms as corresponding secretary, editor, and choir director for college sorority.

- Won national recognition for scrapbook layout, design, and content.

- Contributed quarterly feature and chapter highlights articles to national publication.

## HONORS

- Alpha Lambda Delta Freshman Scholastic Honorary.

- Sigma Delta Chi Journalism Honorary.

- Skull and Crescent Leadership Honorary.

- Worthington Area Panhellenic Scholarship Award (two years).

## Junior product manager

Gretchen Grunig
76 Scotland St.
Standish, ME 04084
207-555-1111

**Career objective:** A position as a junior product manager at aconsumer goods product company.

### Summary

Completing degree in journalism, specializing in marketing at University of Maine. Interned as an assistant account executive (with copywriting responsibilities) for advertising agency. Sold advertising space and supervised staff of three on college newspaper.

### Experience

- Summers, 1999, 2000: Intern, R. Newman Associates, Inc.
- Summer, 1998: Intern, Committee to re-elect Barbara Smith.
- 1998/99 school year: Ad Director, *The Daily Planet*.
- 1997/98 school year: Salesperson, University Book Store.

### Education

B.A. in Journalism with minor in Marketing, University of Maine, 2001.

### Professional memberships and business skills

- Young Professionals Division of the Advertising Club of Maine.
- American Marketing Association (student chapter).

### Skills

- Sales, media placement, typing (50 wpm), familiarity with computers.
- Fluent (read/write/speak) in German and French.

## Computer programmer/analyst

Kimberly Brown
1558 Albany Ave.
St. Paul, MN 55108
612 644-6408

Professional
Qualifications    * Highly dedicated new graduate with well-developed communica-
                  tion and organizational skills; strong management experience.
                  * Goal oriented; able to make effective use of all available resources.
                  * Self-starter; works well independently or as member of a team.

Education    COLLEGE OF ST. JOSEPH, St. Benedict, MN
             **Bachelor of Arts Degree,** May 2000
             Liberal Studies major.
             Advanced coursework in SCIENCE and MANAGEMENT:
             * Microbiology, Chemistry, Anatomy
             * Management, Marketing, Business

Related       VETERAN'S ADMINISTRATION HOSPITAL, St. Benedict, MN
Experience    **Administrative Internship,** February 2000 to May 2000
              * Independently researched and designed a Total Quality Improve-
                ment directory which was approved and implemented by the hospi-
                tal. This same directory was subsequently adapted for official use in
                St. Joseph's Nursing Program.
              * Reviewed and analyzed the hospital's committee system, focusing
                on issues related to member participation, ability to implement
                change, and committee's status (regulation mandated, etc.).

              CARSON PIRIE SCOTT, St. Benedict, MN
              **Sales Associate** – SHOE DEPARTMENT January 2000-present
              * Provide immediate and attentive customer service, assisting with
                selections of moderate to better shoes and accessories.
              * Additional responsibilites include stocking, inventory, balancing
                cash registers, and answering customer questions.

Continuing    VETERAN'S ADMINISTRATION: Ongoing training in VA adminis-
Education     trative, staffing, and committee structures, lines of communication,
              and authority.

Community     Active participant in VISTO, a St. Joseph's sponsored service organi-
              zation.
              Assisted latchkey program at Kennedy Elementary

## Electronics technician (night school student)

RONALD W. WATSON
18828 West Highway
Seattle, WA 98109
(206) 555-9688

**OBJECTIVE:** Position as electronics technician that will utilize technical and supervisory skills developed through military service and part-time employment.

**WORK EXPERIENCE:**

1997-present BOEING AEROSPACE, Seattle, WA
            Special Project Mechanic

- Worked on three projects simultaneously: AWACS, Air Launch Cruise Missile, and Minuteman Missile.
- Installed sensitive electronic communication equipment.
- Assembled the sub-assemblies.
- Assembled and installed various associated components.

**MILITARY EXPERIENCE:**

1997-1997   UNITED STATES NAVY
            Weapons Technician, E-5 (Petty Officer)

- In charge of guidance and control test section.
- Responsible for preventive and corrective maintenance on nuclear weapons systems and components.
- Maintained necessary records.
- Ordered parts, tools, and supplies.
- Inventoried components and test equipment.
- Supervised personnel.
- Operated launchers.
- Served as member of damage control party, firefighting party, and NBC defense team.
- Collateral duties included Naval Courier and explosives driver.

**EDUCATION/ TRAINING:**

UNIVERSITY OF WASHINGTON
Currently working toward B.S. degree in Electrical Engineering.
Degree expected June, 2001.

UNIVERSITY OF MARYLAND, FAR EAST DIVISION
English and Science (48 units).

## Financial planner

### Karen Wolfson

**Until May 22, 2001**
409 Ivy Street
Ypsilanti, MI 48197
313-555-9876

**After May 22, 2001**
27 Wildwood Terrace
Hillsborough, CA 94010
415-555-7592

## Summary of qualifications

Will receive Bachelor's Degree in Finance in May 2001. Extensive knowledge of foreign currency exchange, global finance, cash flow analysis, and other corporate treasury functions.

## Skills

- Extensive knowledge of the Monex treasury workstation.
- Designed and programmed inventory control and reporting systems for classroom project.
- Experience with Quattro and other PC-based spreadsheet programs.

## Education

B.S. in Finance, Ypsilanti State College, College Town, MI.
Graduation Date: May 2001. GPA to date: 3.74/4.0

## Leadership experience

**President,** Omega Alpha Omega Fraternity,  1999-2000.
- Served as liaison between local chapter and national officers.
- Coordinated national leadership school, organizing seminars, and workshops for regional chapter officers.

**Editor,** 2000-2001.
- Wrote and edited articles for national fraternity newsletter.

## Honors and awards

Ypsilanti State Scholarship Recipient, 1997.

Karlheinz Stockhausen Outstanding Paper Award Winner, 1999.

## Employment history

Phillipe Maurice Finance Department; intern, 1999-2000, summers.
Key Food Supermarkets, Mill Valley, CA, cashier, 1997-1998, summers.

## Publishing researcher

### Kristen Lynn Jamel
**220 Broadway Avenue**
**Easton, PA  18042**
**610-555-6145**

**OBJECTIVE:**  Use research and administrative skills to provide background material for feature writers at a major newspaper or magazine publishing company.

**EDUCATION:**  Pennsylvania State University, B.A. June 1999

- Major: English (Writing Option).
- Minor: Journalism and Philosophy.
- GPA 3.7; Class rank, 189/2,107.
- Head of research for school paper 1997-1999.
- Played three varsity sports for four years.
- All-American 2nd team, soccer, 1999.

**EXPERIENCE:**

1997-1999          **WRSC Radio,** State College, PA (25 hours/week)

- Gather, write, and produce news for campus radio station.
- Write and produce features on State College athletes and coaches, both men and women.
- Organized and developed community-oriented program on Women's Equality Day.

1996          **Easton Times-Herald,** Easton, PA (summer)

- Assisted head of Research Department.
- Worked with a variety of reporters and freelance feature writers, providing background and detailed information when required.

## Social worker

Judy Halter
47 Oak Tree Street
Clinton, MO 64735
816-555-1199

### OBJECTIVE

To serve as a children's caseworker in a public or private hospital.

### EDUCATION

B.S.W., Southern Missouri State College, Springfield, MO, 1999.
Concentrated training in social work with emphasis on psychiatric and
pediatric care.

### WORK EXPERIENCE

**Family Caseworker**, Kansas City State Hospital, Kansas City, MO
Sept. 1997 to present

Interview members of families at the hospital or in their homes to help
them adjust to social/economic situations. Developed patient family
transition program that hospital adopted after a two-month pilot.

**Hospital Aide**, Riley Hospital, Indianapolis, IN
Sept. 1995 to May 1997

Assisted administrators with entertainment and recreational programs for
young patients at children's hospital.

### PROFESSIONAL AFFILIATIONS

National Association of Social Workers
National Caseworkers Association

## Advertising (working toward graduate degree)

### Laura Fitzgerald

**Home address:**
80 Stemmons Freeway
Dallas, TX 75260
(214) 555-7880

**School address:**
4240 Hill Street
Carson, CA 90774
(310) 555-0100

JOB OBJECTIVE:    An advertising research position.

EDUCATION:

**University of California, Los Angeles**
Completing course work and thesis for master's degree
in Marketing, June 2001. Graduate courses in
advertising theory and policies, consumer behavioral
theory, sales management.

B.A. degree in Marketing. Dean's List four years;
Summa cum laude.
Fields of study include marketing and advertising
theory, research, business law, economics, statistical
analysis, and research methodology.

**Greg Wright High School**, Los Angeles, CA
National Honor Society, Senior Class President,
United Way Club Head Fund Raiser.

EXPERIENCE:
1999-2000

**JIM CANNON, INC.,** Los Angeles, CA
Administrative assistant in Research Department.
Trained (summers) in behavioral research tecniques.
Responsible for record keeping, expense reports,
public relations, lab report dissemination
correspondence.

1998-1999

**KISCHTRONICS,** San Diego, CA,
Basic sales and management training at this major
research and development facility. Duties included
billing, inventory control, shipping and distribution,
lab maintenance, and delivery schedules.

## Civil engineer

FRANK LAPLACA

2176 Delmar Avenue, #4823

Peoria, IL 61601

309-555-8600

**OBJECTIVE:** An entry-level position offering an opportunity for growth in the civil engineering field.

**EDUCATION:** Illinois Institute of Technology

Bachelor of Science in Civil Engineering, 2001

Major GPA; 3.58/4.00; Overall GPA: 3.48/4.00

**COURSE WORK:**

| In Major (semester hours) | Supporting Courses |
|---|---|
| Strength of Materials (4) | Mathematics (17) |
| Fluid Mechanics (4) | Physics (11) |
| Structural Analysis (3) | Chemistry (15) |
| Reinforced Concrete (4) | Geology (5) |
| Transportation Engineering (3) | English (9) |
| Pavement Design (3) | Surveying (4) |
| Soil Mechanics (4) | Psychology (3) |
| Advanced Soil Mechanics (3) | Economics (7) |
| Structural Steel Design (4) | Humanities (9) |

**RESEARCH EXPERIENCE:** Dr. James Whitney, Professor in Structural Design Illinois Institute of Technology, Fall 1999

- Statics problem: Produced solutions for a new statics book. Worked on more than 100 problems.

- Concrete beam: Worked on computer program dealing with analysis and design of concrete beams.

Frank LaPlaca
page -2-

**RESEARCH
EXPERIENCE:**
(continued)

Dr. Floyd Davis, Assistant Professor/Civil Engineering
Illinois Institute of Technology, Spring 1998

- Seepage problem: Worked on a computer program
  dealing with two-dimensional seepage under a
  sheet piling.

- Embankment loading: Worked on a computer
  program that will be used to determine the stress
  distribution under an embankment loading.

**HONORS &
ACTIVITIES:**

Dean's List, Fall 1999
Chi Epsilon, Civil Engineering Honor Society (Member)
International Students Advisory Board (Member)
American Society of Civil Engineers (Associate Member)

## Petroleum engineer

# ERIC SPRAY

**Permanent address:**
2201 Bourbon Street
Broad Run, VA 22014
(703) 555-2081

**Temporary address:**
119 Clark Ave., #9
Austin, TX 78710
(512) 555-7666

## PROFESSIONAL OBJECTIVE

To obtain an entry-level position in the operational areas of
petroleum engineering at a major oil company.

## EDUCATION

THE UNIVERSITY OF TEXAS AT AUSTIN
Baccalaureate Candidate in Petroleum Engineering
Degree expected May, 2001.

## ACADEMIC PROFILE

Completed courses:

- Reservoir Engineering
- Applied Reservoir Engineering
- Applied Reservoir Analysis
- Reservoir Modeling
- Engineering Secondary Recovery
- Formation Evaluation
- Petroleum Engineering Design
- Well Treating and Evaluation
- Rock and Fluid Lab
- Oil Well Drilling
- Drilling Design & Production

## WORK EXPERIENCE

**SUPERVISOR**—SEARS WAREHOUSE, Austin, TX
(part-time summer employment) 1998 and 1999.

- Supervised five warehouse employees during the night shift.

Spray
page 2

**ASSISTANT DEPARTMENT MANAGER**—KMART, Austin, TX
(part-time during school year; approx. 20 hours/week) 1999 and 2000.

- Responsible for overall maintenance as well as scheduling and supervision of four part-time employees in housewares department.
- Revised merchandise layout and recommended changes that resulted in increased product visibility.

**LAB ASSISTANT**—UNIVERSITY OF TEXAS, Austin, TX

(part-time during school year; approx. 25 hours/week) 1997 and 1998.
- Worked in the Instrumentation Lab and assisted in the development of a Phase Comparator system for the study of plasma physics.
- Designed an active band-pass filter circuit with predictable phase response.

### ACTIVITIES/ACCOMPLISHMENTS

- Member of the Society of Petroleum Engineers.
- Member of the Engineering Club.
- Working knowledge of INTERACT, CMS, and IBM PC computers.

## Materials engineer

**Anthony Rutigliano**
33 Fairview Blvd., Apt. 6
Madison, WI 53717
608-555-2003

**Profile**

Skilled research engineer with doctorate in materials engineering. Strong background in manufacturing process development and in product improvement programs. Experienced in managing projects from conception to completion.

**Education**

**Doctorate of Philosophy**
**University of Wisconsin - Madison (2000)**
Dissertation topic: Alloy modifications to Deotel 61 to reduce additions of strategic elements while retaining the original material properties.

**Master of Science**
**Massachusetts Institute of Technology (1997)**
Thesis topic: Optimizing the structure and properties of advanced cast irons to improve thermal fatigue resistance.

**Bachelor of Science**
**New York University (1995)**

**Publications**

**Doctoral Dissertation**
Rutigliano, *Metallurgy and Properties Research*, Pressman Publishers, 2001.

**Master's Thesis**
Rutigliano, *National Foundryman's Journal*, Wolcott & Associates, 1998.

Rutigliano
Page 2

**Invited Paper/ Presentation**

"Improved Product Performance Through Application of High-Strength Steels, Advanced Aluminum Alloys, Metal and Polymer Composites and Ceramics," 1998 International Tool Manufacturing Show, New York City, NY.

**Experience**

**Professor's Assistant, Massachusetts Institute of Technology (September 1995-May 1997)**
Assisted and instructed undergraduate students in classroom and laboratory settings.

- Created all lecture, semester, and final exam materials.
- Helped revise curriculum and graduation requirements for materials engineering students to better prepare them for the job market.

## Electrical engineer

**Lawrence Aronson**
1500 Dunes Circle
Redlands, CA 92373
(714) 555-1026

**OBJECTIVE:** A technical position which utilizes my educational and technical background in electrical engineering and mathematics

**EDUCATION:** University of California, Davis
B.S. Electrical Engineering expected June 2001
GPA 3.5

Electrical Engineering course work: Basic Electrical and Electronic Circuits; Circuit Theories I & II; Circuit Analysis Laboratory; Electronics I & II and corresponding laboratory work; Feedback Control Systems

System Science course work: Stochastic Processes; Probability; Statistics I & II; Applied Numerical Computing; Linear Programming

Mathematics course work: Real Analysis I & II; Fourier and Laplace Transfers; Linear Algebra; Mathematical Modeling

**EXPERIENCE:** Lockheed Missiles and Space Company (Summer 1999) Worked with the statistics and parts engineering groups on various assignments relating to the long term degradation of stored Trident 1 missile parts. Work included trend analyses, warehouse inspections, and programming in DPL.

**SKILLS:** Programming experience with Pascal and DPL. Have used the UNIX, Sylbur, and Executive Operating Systems on various mainframes. Experience with the WordStar operating system on the IBM PC and SPICE for analyzing electronic circuits.

**ACTIVITIES:** Member, Circuits and Systems Society
President, Sigma Nu Fraternity

## Typist-office clerk

Melinda Scarso
12201 Virginia Way
Danbury, CT 06810
203-555-9146

**OBJECTIVE:**

To provide top-quality, conscientious service as typist and office clerk in a New York City industrial firm.

**EXPERIENCE:**

1992-1995

**Typist, File Clerk**

Feinberg Associates, Danbury, CT

Assembled data from legal reports, typed revisions and legal contracts, served as relief receptionist, maintained files, and provided general office assistance.

1989-1992

**Typist-Receptionist**

Manzo Realtors, Forest Hills, NY

Served as receptionist to large real estate company: typed documents related to sale and purchase of property; filed records of clients and construction companies; main tained appointment schedules.

**EDUCATION:**

Graduated with commercial diploma from Danbury High School, June 1989.

**OFFICE SKILLS:**

Typing—75 wpm; shorthand—100 wpm; Familiar with Windows and Excel for both IBM and Apple PCs.

## High School Science Teacher

Melinda Manley
28 Prairie Lane
Fargo, ND 58102
701-555-3002

**OBJECTIVE:** Looking for the opportunity to generate excitement and interest in the sciences and help junior and senior high school students develop academically, socially, and personally.

**SKILLS PROFILE:**
- Experienced in creating lesson plans, designing lab experiments, and maintaining disciplined atmosphere.
- Knowledgeable in designing and evaluating computer science labs.
- Strong volunteer/instructional background.
- Experienced in working with children of all ages.
- Excellent rapport with students.
- Skilled in successful fund raising, event planning, and program development.
- Experienced in Pascal and Basic computer programming.

**EDUCATION**

1995-current     Graduate studies, North Dakota State University

1985     Endorsements in General Sciences and Physical Sciences, North Dakota State University

1985     B.S. in Biology, with honors
North Dakota State University

**STUDENT TEACHING**

Sept.-Dec. 1984     **Student Teacher, Marshall High School
Marshall, ND**
- Taught first-year biology and chemistry.
- Assisted in second-year biology.
- Created a contact system for grades on one unit, resulting in higher achievement and lab and test scores.
- Created all daily lessons, tests, laboratory experiments, and semester tests for both biology and chemistry.

Manley
page 2

## INSTRUCTIONAL EXPERIENCE

1995-current    **Substitute Teacher, Fargo Jr./Sr. High School
Fargo, ND**

- Instruct students in all subject areas.
- Complete lesson plans as directed and provide teacher with feedback.
- Maintain disciplined academic atmosphere.

1993-current    **Volunteer Science Instructor, Fargo Community
School Corp., Fargo, ND**

- Assist, instruct, and provide feedback to junior and senior high school students on a variety of lab projects.
- Work with students on defining their research and hypotheses and determining their variables for successful science fair projects.

1990-1993    **Church School Teacher/Vacation Bible School
Teacher, First United Presbyterian Church,
Fargo, ND**

- Instructed elementary and preschool children each Sunday and during week-long summer Bible school sessions.
- Created lesson plans and designed related activities.

1985-1987    **Science Teacher, Prairie High School
Bismarck, ND**

- Taught first-year biology and second-year chemistry students.
- Coordinated annual science fair and guided students in their research and development of successful projects.

## VOLUNTEER EXPERIENCE

1993-current    **Member, Textbook Adoption Committee
Fargo Community School, Fargo, ND**

- Review elementary-level English, science, and mathematics textbooks and recommend which should be included in curriculum.

1994-1995    **Officer, Fargo Elementary Parent/Teacher
Organization Fargo, ND**

- Organized most successful fund-raising carnival to date.
- Planned first-ever T-shirt sales program.

## Management trainee (returning serviceman)

ADAM WALLACE
607 North Lakeland Drive
Memphis, TN 38119
(901) 555-0202

**JOB OBJECTIVE**
To secure a management trainee position with a large consumer-products company.

**MILITARY SERVICE**

**U.S. Navy Apprentice Seaman promoted to Seaman 1st Class**
(June 1995 to June 2000)

- Stationed in Alaska.

- Honorably discharged.

**BUSINESS EXPERIENCE**

**Management Trainee, W.T. Grant, Nashville, TN**
(August 1993 to May 1995)

- Assisted customers in every department of the store.

- Operated the cash registers.

- Supervised stock room.

- Tracked inventory of merchandise in stock.

**EDUCATION**
Nashville Commercial High School, Nashville, TN (1989 to 1993).

**OTHER ACTIVITIES**

- Member, Big Brothers of Memphis, a volunteer organization that helps young boys without fathers.

- Coach, Memphis Spring Soccer League.

## Military entering work force

THOMAS T. CAMPANELLI
315 Magnolia Drive
Deerfield Beach, FL 33441
305-555-1664

SKILLS
PROFILE

Ten years aeronautical and engineering experience, including obtaining five commercial and experimental patents. Skilled in developing methods that have become Air Force standards. Solid background in computer and software operations, budget and personnel management, and training.

WORK
EXPERIENCE

8/98-present

**Air Force Flight Test Center, Samuels Air ForceBase, FL. Captain/Flight Commander**

Program manager for testing and evaluating integrated software systems on F-15 aircraft. F-15 airborne test director and weapon system operator

- Managed schedule and costs within budget of approximately $14M per year.

- Supervised 17 engineers and three technicians, wrote performance evaluations and oversaw training.

- Saved $120K in annual costs through cross-training.

- Developed original methods for weapons accuracy analysis, which was published and presented at professional conference and recommended for Air Force standard.

5/96-8/98

**Air Force Flight Test Center, Samuels Air Force Base, FL. Captain/Lead Avionics Engineer**

Prepared technical and safety flight test plans, reviewed and approved technical reports of test results, and authorized specific flight profiles.

- Directed hazardous, low-level flight program with no safety incidents.

- Wrote published standards of radar altimeter suitability as test data source.

- Implemented computerized data base to control aircraft software configuration.

Campanelli
page 2

6/91-8/93    **Shuttle Test Group, Williams Air Force Base, CA.
Lieutenant/Mechanisms Engineer**

Served with unit providing Air Force support for Space
Shuttle operations.

- Console-certified engineer for pre-launch processing
  and launch operations.

- Member of Kennedy Space Center launch control
  room team for four launches

EDUCATION    **United States Air Force Test Pilot School,
Williams Air Force Base, CA (1996)**

**Air Force Institute of Technology
Dayton, OH (1995)**

- Masters of Science in Aeronautical Engineering

- Awarded joint patent on experimental nozzle design

**Syracuse University, Syracuse, NY (1991)**

- Bachelor of Arts in Engineering Science

- Received joint patent on commercial electro-
  mechanical design

CURRENT      Captain, United States Air Force Reserve
STATUS       (Clearance: Secret)

AWARDS       Meritorious Service Medal for Operation Desert Storm
                 deployment

             1998 Outstanding Volunteer, Deerfield Beach Girls' and
                 Boys' Club

ACTIVITIES   Volunteer/Basketball Coach, Deerfield Beach Girls' and
                 Boys' Club (1996-present)

             Project Leader, Eagle Scout Radio-Controlled Airplane
                 project  (1996-present)

## Teacher (military entering different field)

PAUL OTTENS
39 Citation Circle
Ames, IA 50010
515-555-6887

CAREER OBJECTIVE      A position as a secondary teacher.

SKILLS SUMMARY        Manager, engineer, and instructor with extensive
                      background in operations, leadership, instruction,
                      and training. Demonstrated ability to successfully
                      train and lead up to 1,800-person unit. Solid
                      education in instructional techniques. Licensed
                      teacher in the state of Iowa.

EDUCATION             **Iowa State University, Ames, IA (1993-1995)**
                      Undergraduate courses to fulfill teaching certificate
                      requirements

                      **U.S. Military Academy, West Point, NY (1984)**
                      Bachelor of Science in Engineering

PROFESSIONAL
STUDIES               **Officer Basic and Advanced Course (1986)**
                      18-month post-graduate schooling that included
                      lesson plan preparation, instruction, and training
                      techniques

                      **Combined Arms Staff College (1987)**
                      Senior officer schooling focusing on staff and
                      administrative functions and covering advanced
                      briefing and instructional techniques

LICENSING             Secondary Education Teaching Certificate,
                      State of Iowa (1995)

INSTRUCTIONAL EXPERIENCE
1995-present          **Substitute Teacher, Ames Public School System,
                      Ames, IA**
                      Complete a variety of assignments, including 12-
                      week assignment in high school biology and
                      chemistry classes.

Ottens
page 2

- Created special unit for history curriculum on Desert Storm and its significance in U.S. military history.

1990-1992

**Operations Manager, U.S. Army, Dhahran, Saudi Arabia**

Handled all operations and training of 1,800-person logistics unit that provided supplies for Middle East. Tour of duty included Operation Desert Storm.
- Unit commended by General Schwartzkopf.
- Demonstrated ability to rapidly create and execute team training program under demanding conditions.

1989-1990

**Commander, U.S. Army, West Germany**

Managed 150-person unit.
- Administered training program that effectively taught individual, collective, and multi-echelon (various level of command) skills to produce a combat-ready unit.

1985-1989

**Training Officer, U.S. Army, California and West Germany**

Served as training supervisor for 125-person unit and training manager for 500-person unit.
- Handled hands-on teaching and curriculum development.
- Created alternative means of assessment, which more accurately identified accomplishments and areas needing improvement.

1984

**Cadet Basic Training Squad Leader and Platoon Leader, U.S. Military Academy, West Point, NY**

Taught and led unique and exciting eight-week educational experience.
- Served on team that transformed a culturally and educationally diverse freshman class into acohesive group of young men and women, prepared for the rigors of cadet life.

ACTIVITIES

Volunteer Tutor, Carnegie Public Library, Ames, IA
Boy Scout Leader, Troop 121, Ames, IA

# Food services manager (no paid experience)

**Eve Mossman**
463 S 240 E
Decatur, IN 47633
219-555-8746

CAREER GOAL:

A position as a food services manager or catering supervisor.

EXPERIENCE:

**Organizational/management skills**

- Organize, host, plan menu, and supervise preparation of all food for 500 guests at annual Indiana Cattle Association picnic (23 years).
- Organize 120 volunteers and supervise food preparation for State Fair beef tent, which brings in $100,000 annually for the State Cattle Association (10 years).
- Chair meal portion of home economics club's annual fall bazaar and luncheon, including purchasing goods and supervising food preparation; for eight years have consistently brought food purchases in under budget and exceeded fund-raising goals by 20%.

**Financial/budgeting skills**

- Skilled in handling computerized bookkeeping for 1,200-acre grain and 250 head cattle farming operation.
- Initiated and completed data entry from manual to computerized system, resulting in improved account analysis, improved report generation for loan/banking and tax purposes, and reduced bookkeeping time.
- Experienced in monthly farm and household budgeting and timely payment of personal and business accounts.

**Other related skills**

- Experienced in planning and creating low-fat, low-sugar, and low-sodium meals.
- Skilled in presenting knowledgeable instruction on proper food handling and storage.

EDUCATION:

Bachelor of Science in Home Economics
Purdue University, West Lafayette, IN

MEMBERSHIPS:

President, Secretary, Treasurer, Out and About Home Ec Club, Warren County, IN

President, Treasurer, United Methodist Women, United Methodist Church, Decatur, IN

## Fund raiser (volunteer experience)

### ELLEN MEYER-SCHORB

57 Brandon Street · Gloucester, NC · 28528 · 919-555-8750

### OBJECTIVE

A position as a fund raiser for a nonprofit organization.

### SKILLS/ABILITIES

#### Management/Organization

- Served two terms as president of philanthropic group; increased membership 30%; established new fund raiser that brought in $1,500 annually to benefit the community.
- Served as secretary for school Parent/Teacher Organization for two years.
- Chaired and organized PTO school carnival, which raised $2,500 and was the most successful fund-raising event in 10 years.
- Assisted in coordinating volunteer drivers for senior services organization.

#### Teaching/Training

- Tutored (through library program) four first- and second-grade students in reading.
- Hosted story hour with children's librarian at local public library, including scheduling special guests and organizing visits to the police and fire departments, post office, and more.

#### Communication/Leadership

- Developed and distributed brochures for local public library about children's programs, which nearly doubled attendance at the programs.
- Served on team with representatives from county agencies to develop and implement childcare provider training and certification program to improve the quality of childcare offered in private homes.

### VOLUNTEER WORK HISTORY

Gloucester Public Library, Children's Department, Tutoring Department, Gloucester, NC (1992-present)

Gloucester Public Schools, Parent/Teacher Organization, Gloucester, NC (1994-present)

County Youth Coalition, Child Care Services Team, Gloucester, NC (1995-present)

Psi Iota Xi national philanthropic society, Omega Chapter, Gloucester, NC (1994-1995)

### EDUCATION

Bachelor of Arts in Consumer and Family Sciences, Indiana State University, Terre Haute, IN (1985)

# Publicity (returning to work force)

Kimberly Schand
259 Gruber Lane
Lake Oswego, OR 97035
503-555-1234

## QUALIFICATIONS SUMMARY

More than 16 years experience in publicity, communication, and promotions. Direct all promotional activity for membership events that involve hundreds of attendees. Planned all aspects of semi-annual training seminars for groups of more than 100.

## EXPERIENCE

1993-present    Vice President, Membership, regional council of Women's American Organization for Rehabilitation Through Training Lake Oswego, OR.

- Direct membership operations for three area chapters of international fund-raising organization.

- Initiate and plan membership drives and other membership recruiting events.

- Computerized all membership records, which streamlined mailing operations and reduced costs by 20%.

1991-1993    President, local chapter, Women's American ORT Lake Oswego, OR.

- Administered chapter operations, including programs,fund raising, and communications. Supervised 15-member executive board.

- Introduced and implemented new promoting that increased funds by 40% in one year.

- During two-year term, increased chapter membership by 25%.

1987-1992    Chairman, Camp Committee, Community Center Lake Oswego, OR.

- Led committee that developed day camp policies and promoted summer camp enrollment.

1985-1991    Director of Marketing, Lake Credit Union Lake Oswego, OR.

- Instituted comprehensive marketing program for $16 million credit union.

- Developed, wrote, and edited bimonthly membernewsletter.

Schand
Page 2

- Supervised all marketing activity and a staff of six.

**1981-1984**     Director of Public Relations, Lake Credit Union.
Lake Oswego, OR

- Established and directed marketing program for $20 million credit union.

- Wrote, edited and produced bimonthly newsletter.

- Developed and implemented system for internal communications among six field offices.

**1977-1981**     Administrator, Center for Adult Learning
Lake Oswego, OR.

- Designed courses for adult, post-secondary students.

## EDUCATION

**1978**     M.S. Design and Management of Post-Secondary Education, University of Wisconsin, Madison.

**1976**     B.S. Elementary Education, Rutgers University, New Brunswick, NJ.

## COMPUTER SKILLS

- Familiar with IBM-compatible and Macintosh systems.

- Experience with word processing programs, including WordPerfect and Microsoft Word.

- Knowledge of graphics and analytical tools, including Harvard Graphics and Lotus 1-2-3.

# Sales (reentering work force)

LAUREN PALAZZI
503 Van Buren Street
Paramus, NJ 07652
201-555-7890

## Skills Summary

More than 12 years sales and marketing experience in professional and volunteer positions. Solid telephone sales background; planned and administered successful telephone fund-raising campaigns.

## Sales Experience

- Telephone fund raiser for charity campaign benefiting underprivileged children. Achieved highest individual goal three years in a row.
- Chairman of sales for annual fundraising project benefiting high school band. Surpassed sales goals this year by $1,000.
- Sales manager of nonprofit boutique selling school supplies and specialty items.

## Leadership Experience

- Chaired women's division of annual charity fund-raising drive; directed phone solicitation efforts of 100 volunteers.
- Supervised staff of 15 adult volunteer salespeople working in nonprofit boutique.

## Organizational Experience

- Coordinated facilities and solicited volunteers for three-day telephone fund raiser that raised $5 million in donations for local charity.
- Administered day-to-day activities in school-operated boutique; maintained inventory, ordered merchandise, and scheduled volunteer sales staff.

## Professional and Volunteer Work History

| | |
|---|---|
| 1993-1995 | Committee chair, Old Birch High School PTA, Dallas, TX |
| 1980-1982 | Salesperson, Loretta's Fine Jewelry, Dallas, TX |
| 1973-1975 | Teacher, 1st grade, Ridge Elementary School, Galveston, TX |
| 1969-1973 | Summer camp counselor, Clear Lake Day Camp, Dallas, TX |

## Education

B.S. Elementary Education, University of Texas at Austin, 1973.

## Secretary (homemaker entering work force)

### KATHRYN WOLTER
### 522 Castle Court
### Arkadelphia, AR 71923
### (501) 555-7890

### Job Objective
Secretary in a residence for handicapped adults.

### Skills Summary
12 years experience providing office support in a residence for handicapped children. Excellent office skills, including word processing, typing (80 wpm), filing, and familiarity with medical insurance processing. Strong experience in caregiving for senior citizens and children.

### Office and Organizational Experience
- Initiated reorganization of file system that made patient information more accessible to staff of group home.
- Maintain and update patient files for group home with 150 full-time residents.
- Complete and process medical and dental insurance claim forms.

### Computer Experience
- Trained administrators and therapists at group home on Lotus 1-2-3, saving outside training expenses of more than $1,000.
- Developed and maintained budget program for personal finance.
- Operational knowledge of Apple, Macintosh, and IBM computers.

### Social Services Experience
- Handled personal care and finances of elderly woman for three years.
- Served hot meals to elderly in their homes for eight years.
- Supervise preschool children at church day care.

### Volunteer Work History
- Office support, Florence House Children's Center, Arkadelphia, 1990-present.
- Preschool day-care supervisor, Temple Sholom, Arkadelphia, 1985-present.
- Driver/server, Meals on Wheels, Arkadelphia, 1987-1995.

### Awards and Honors
Volunteer of the Year, Florence House Children's Center, 1999.
Awarded for outstanding service to center for handicapped children.

# Child care worker/teacher (part-time position)

**Jennifer Johns**
**136 Main Street**
**Apple Hill, NJ 07000**
**609-634-1122**

**Objective**    A part-time position utilizing strong organizational, interpersonal, and communication skills

**Qualifications**  Extensive experience in supervising children, including:
- Developing and organizing activites
- Creating arts and crafts projects
- Improving skills
- Motivating students

## EXPERIENCE

**ABC SCHOOL**, Pennsauken, NJ        **2000**
**Student Teacher**
Formulated lesson plans, created bulletin boards, taught third grade in a self-contained classroom, and improved classroom management.
- Designed learning centers to increase students' awareness of the learning process.

**DEFG SCHOOL**, Mt. Laurel, NJ        **1999**
**Student Practicum**
Performed all duties associated with teaching fifth grade in a self-contained classroom and observed teacher-student interaction.

**SUND DAY CAMP**, Medford, NJ    **Summers, 1994 - 1999**
**Senior Counselor**        1997 - 1999
Supervised 18 eight to nine-year-old campers. Planned and organized activities, conducted conferences with parents, initiated innovative programming, and strengthened coordination skills.
- Selected as "Color War" Captain to plan and implement a 22-team athletic competition.

**Junior Counselor**        1994-1996
Assisted senior counselors in coordinating all camp activities.

## EDUCATION

**B.A., Elementary Education, Rowan University,** Glassboro, NJ  2000
**G.P.A 3.2/4.0**
Currently enrolled in Master's Degree Program at **Rowan University**

## Camp counselor (summer position)

Marvin Hagler
185 Spruce Street
Concord, MA 01742
(508) 555-2286

**OBJECTIVE:**

To secure a position for the summer of 2002 as an athletic or senior counselor.

**QUALIFICATIONS:**

- Full Red Cross training
- Life Saving Certificate, Class IV
- CPR Certification
- Seven letters in high school sports

**EDUCATION:**

Junior, the University of Pennsylvania Majoring in Political Science

**EXPERIENCE:**

Athletic Counselor, Camp Win-A-Poo, Elmira, NY summers 1998 and 1999

- Responsible for all sports for the 12- to 16-year old age group—sports included swimming, tennis, archery, and horseback riding.
- Supervised four junior counselors.
- Worked under Chief Counselor—responsible for all sports and activities scheduling.

# Chapter 11

# The Lost Art of Letter Writing

People used to write letters. Lots of them. Just look through some of the shelves at your local library. You'll find a surprising number of collections of letters—between literary figures, political figures, philosophers, theologians, and, of course, the intimate letters from husband to wife, lover to lover, friend to friend.

Presuming you were part of the "literate class," the fundamentals of letter writing were learned at home, part of the growing up process. Letters were the only way to keep in touch with anyone who lived more than a day away. So letter writing, while art to some, was vital to most.

In our age of instant communication, in which the telephone, fax, e-mail, and Instant Messenger long ago replaced the pen, the average person devotes far less time to letter writing than ever. Most letters are now simply mailbox clutter—impersonal junk mail. As a result, it is essential that I include a chapter on the fundamentals of letter writing, surely one of the most important skills to be mastered in the job search process. (In fact, in some instances, a well-crafted cover letter may be more important than your resume!)

## You are what you write

Stop for a moment and review your resume draft. If you've followed my advice, it is undoubtedly a near-perfect document that instantly tells the reader the kind of job you want and why you are qualified. But does it say anything personal about you? Any amplification of your talents? Any words that are ideally "you"? Any hint of the kind of person who stands behind that resume?

If you've prepared it properly, the answers should be a series of ringing "no's." Your resume should be a mere sketch of your life, a bare-bones summary of your skills, education, and experience.

To this general sketch we must add the details—the lines, colors, and shading that will help fill out your self-portrait. This chapter will cover, in detail, the kinds of letters you will most often be called upon to prepare during your job search.

# Answer these questions

Before you compose any letter, ask yourself these five key questions:

1. **Why** are you writing it?
2. To **whom** are you writing it?
3. **What** are you trying to accomplish?
4. **Which** lead will grab your reader's attention?
5. **How** should you organize your letter to best accomplish your objectives?

## *Why?*

There should be a single, easily definable reason you are writing any letter. This reason will often dictate what and how you write—the "tone" of the letter—as well as what you include or leave out.

If you've been asked in an ad to list your qualifications for a job, provide a salary history, and portfolio samples, that (minimally) is your objective in writing. Limit yourself to following instructions and a little "selling"—very little.

If, however, you are in the process of building a job search network, the objective of your letter is to seek out contacts that will refer you for possible informational or job interviews. In this case, getting a name and address—a referral—is your stated purpose for writing. You have to be specific and ask for this action.

## *To whom?*

Properly addressing the person to whom you are writing and using an appropriate "tone" is as important as what you say to them.

For example, it pays to sound technical with technical people—to use the kinds of words and language that they use on the job. If you have had the opportunity to speak with someone, this task will be much easier for you. The cardinal rule is to say it in words you think the recipient will be comfortable hearing, not in the words you might otherwise choose.

## *What?*

What do you have to offer that company? What do you have to contribute to the job or work situation that is unique and/or of particular benefit to the recipient of your letter? For example, if you are applying for a sales position and were recently ranked number one in a summer sales job, then it would be logical to emphasize this accomplishment. Even if you listed it in the skills/accomplishments section of your resume, you can—and should—still call attention to it in your letter. Properly focused repetition is a plus.

## *Which?*

A dynamic opening sentence will quickly grab the reader's attention—and you'll be 50 percent of the way to having your entire letter read. Don't slide into it. Know the point you are trying to make and get right to it.

## How?

While a good opening is essential, the way you organize your letter will determine whether the recipient will read it in its entirety. Is it easy to read? Do the words and sentences naturally lead one to another, holding the reader's interest until he reaches your signature?

If you have your objective clearly in mind, this task is easier than it sounds: Simply convey your message(s) in a logical sequence. End your letter by stating what the next steps are—yours and/or the reader's.

## When to write

- To answer an ad.
- To prospect (many companies).
- To inquire about specific openings (single company).
- To obtain a referral (networking).
- To obtain an informational interview (networking).
- To obtain a job interview.
- To say "thank you" after an informational or job interview.
- To accept or reject a job offer.
- To withdraw from consideration for a job.

I have included at least one sample of each of these letters at the end of this chapter.

## Answering an ad

Your eye catches an ad for an administrative assistant in the Positions Available section of the Sunday paper. It tells you that the position is in a large medical office and that, though some experience would be desirable, it is not required. The ad asks that you send a letter and resume to a post office box. No salary indicated, no phone number given. You decide to reply.

Your objective (the why?) is to secure a job interview. Because no hiring manager has been named and you know from the description that you will be writing to a large company, you must assume your letter will be screened by someone in the Human Resources Department.

You are answering a "blind" ad, so you have to play it safe. Adopt a professional, formal tone. In your first sentence, refer to the ad—including the place and date of publication and the position outlined. (Chances are, this company is running more than one ad on the same date and in the same paper, so you need to identify the one to which you are replying.)

Tell the reader what *specifically* you have to offer that company. Include your resume, phone number, and the times of day it is easiest to reach you. Ask for the order—in other words, tell them you'd like to have an appointment. See page 153 for an example of this type of letter.

# Blanket prospecting letter

In June of this year, you will graduate from a four-year college with a degree in advertising and communications. You seek a position (internship or full-time employment) in a major advertising agency's media department. You have decided to write to 50 advertising agencies, sending each a copy of your resume.

Such blanket mailings can be effective only if: 1) You have an exemplary record and a resume that reflects it; 2) you send out a huge number of packages, since the response rate to such mailings is very low; and 3) you direct each of them to a specific individual.

A blanket mailing doesn't mean an impersonal one—you should always be writing to a specific executive. If you have a referral, send a personalized letter to that person. If not, do not simply mail a package to the Human Resources Department. Identify the department head (you might find the name in one of the directories listed in Chapter 2) and send a personalized letter. Make sure you get on the phone and follow up each letter within about 10 days. An example of a prospecting letter is on page 154.

The growth of online job search and resume-posting sites has made such mass mailings even less effective than in the past. But there are still employers who are uncomfortable online, key players you will miss entirely if you *only* post your resume on the Web.

# Just inquiring

The inquiry letter is a step beyond the blanket prospecting letter; it's a "cold-calling" device—with a twist. Let's say you have targeted a company (and a person) in your job search based on something you have read. Your general research tells you this company would be a good place to work. Although you are not aware of any specific openings, you know that the company employs entry-level personnel with your credentials.

While ostensibly inquiring about any openings, you are really aiming at getting your resume in front of the right person. An example of one of these "shots in the near dark" letters is on page 155.

# Networking

It's time to get out that folder marked "Contacts" and prepare a draft of a networking letter. The lead sentence should be very specific, referring immediately to the friend or colleague "who suggested I write you about..." Remember: Your objective is to secure an informational interview, pave the way for a job interview, and/or get referred to still other contacts.

You will notice in the sample letter on page 156 that a good networking letter does not require the recipient to make a decision about hiring you; rather, the request is couched in terms of "career advice."

Unless you have been specifically asked by the referring person to do so, you will probably not include a resume with a networking letter. So, the letter itself must highlight your credentials, enabling the reader to gauge your level of experience, and, for entry-level job hunters, education.

The letter on page 157 is to request an informational interview with someone to whom you have *not* been referred. So you must convince the reader—with*out* the aid of a "friend of a friend"—of the sincerity of your research effort. A positive response to this type of request is itself a big step forward—you're adding to your contact list and exposing yourself to a new lead.

## Thank-you letters

Although it may not always seem so, manners *do* count in the job world. And the best show of good manners is the small gesture that shows you actually care—writing a thank-you letter. Whatever else your resume tells them, it illustrates that you are, at least, polite, courteous, and thoughtful.

On a more practical level, a thank-you letter might well become the beginning of an all-important dialogue that leads directly to a job. So be especially careful in composing them, and make certain that they are cus-tom-made for each occasion and person. The following are the primary situations in which you will be called upon to write some variation of a thank-you letter:

1. After a job interview.
2. After an informational interview with a network contact.
3. When accepting a job offer.
4. When responding to rejection: While optional, such a letter is appropriate if you have been among the finalists in a job search or were rejected because your experience was limited. Remember: Some day you will *have* enough experience. Make the inter-viewer *want* to stay in touch with you.
5. Withdrawing from consideration: Should you decide that you are no longer interested in a particular position or are declining a job offer, it would be appropriate to send this type of "thanks but no thanks" letter. Whatever the reason for writing such a letter, it's wise to keep future lines of communication open.

## Some final words about style

A letter can perform an entirely different role from that of your re-sume. It can make an argument for you, give you a chance to be creative and convince the recipient that there is a thinking human being attached to an otherwise dry recounting of credentials.

Your resume is a product of research and self-examination. It is a statement of fact—unembellished, brief, and to the point. Your letters should be a product of thought, emotion, and imagination. Despite the fact that I've included sample letters to guide you in your letter writing, there are few hard and fast rules. Of course, they should be neat, grammatically correct, and not overly long—a page will suffice. Other than that, try to imprint each letter you write with your own distinct style. Let them be you.

## In response to an ad

7 Lobell Court
Storrs, CT 06268
February 10, 2001

The New York Times
P.O. Box 7520
New York, NY 10128

Dear Sir or Madam:

This letter is in response to your advertisement for an Administrative Assistant, which appeared in the February 9th issue of *The New York Times*.

I have the qualifications you are seeking. I graduated from Evelyn Woods Secretarial School three months ago. In addition, I have worked as a part-time laboratory assistant at Barnaby Hospital for the past two semesters. This position has provided me with hands-on experience in the medical field and has given me a chance to polish my office administration skills. My resume is enclosed.

I would like to have the opportunity to meet with you personally to discuss your requirements for the position. I can be reached at (203) 555-1225 between 8 a.m. and 5 p.m. and at (203) 555-4221 after 5 p.m. I look forward to hearing from you.

Sincerely,


Brenda Hartley

Enclosure: Resume

## Prospecting letter

Kim Kerr
8 Robutuck Hwy.
Hammond, IN  46325
219-555-6429
kimkerr@mailme.com

June 14, 2001

Mr. Fred Jones, Vice President - Media
Alcott & Alcott
One Lakeshore Drive
Chicago, IL  60611

Dear Mr. Jones:

The name of Alcott & Alcott continually pops up in our classroom discussions about outstanding advertising agencies. Given my interest in advertising as a career, and media as a specialty, I've taken the liberty of enclosing my resume.

As you can see, I have just completed four years of study with concentrations in media planning, media research, demographic targeting, broadcast buying, and plans evaluation. I will be graduating in the top 10 percent of my class, with honors.

My review of the business press, especially *Advertising Age* and *Marketing & Media Decisions*, suggests that, because of your involvement in multimedia, your firm will continue to grow.

I will be in the Chicago area on June 29th and will call your office to see when it is convenient to arrange an appointment.

Sincerely yours,


Kim Kerr


Enclosure: Resume

## Letter of inquiry

42 Woodland Street
Montpelier, VT 05602
May 1, 2001

Ms. Sandra Goodard, President
Recruitment Associates
521 West Elm Street
New Canaan, CT 06840

Dear Ms. Goodard:

I just completed reading the article in *Fortune* magazine on Recruitment Associates. Your innovative approach to recruiting minorities is of particular interest to me because of my background in public relations and minority recruitment.

I am interested in learning more about your work, as well as the possibilities of joining your firm. My qualifications include:

- B.A. in English
- Research on minority recruitment and medical education
- Reports preparation on creative writing, education, and minorities

I will be in Connecticut during the week of October 10 and hope your schedule will permit us to meet briefly to discuss our mutual interests. I will call your office next week to see if such a meeting can be arranged.

I appreciate your consideration.

Sincerely yours,


Marvin Heckler

Enclosure: Resume

## Networking letter

**Francis Rizzo**
**1515 Broadway**
**Minneapolis, MN 55440**
**612-555-9080**
**friz@mmm.com**

June 14, 2001

Mr. Arthur Hyman
Vice President
Engineering Design Associates
42 Jenkins Avenue
Grace, MS 38745

Dear Mr. Hyman:
Our mutual friend, Howard Roach, suggested I write you. I am interested in an entry-level design position with a firm specializing in office construction. Mr. Roach felt it would be mutually beneficial for us to meet and talk.

I have been educated and trained as a draftsman and have just over two years of part-time experience in construction, design, and plan development. I am particularly interested in the construction and design of the kinds of factory projects for which your firm is so well-known.

Mr. Roach mentioned you as one of the leading experts in this field. As I begin my job search during the next few months, I am certain your advice would help me. Would it be possible for us to meet briefly?

I will call your office next week to see when your schedule would permit a meeting.

Sincerely,


Francis Rizzo

## To obtain an informational interview

1497 Lilac Street
Worcester, MA 01602
November 15, 2000

Mr. Michael Lewis
Vice President – Sales
McClure Publishing
485 Smithers Lane
Charleston, S.C. 76857

Dear Mr. Lewis:

I'm sure a great deal of the credit for your company's 27 percent in space sales last year is attributable to the highly motivated sales staff you have recruited during the last three years. I hope to work in such a position for a company just as committed to growth.

I have four years of excellent sales results to boast of, experience acquired while working my way through college. I believe my familiarity with media, sales experience, and B.A. in Communications from American University have properly prepared me for a career in consumer magazine space sales.

As I begin my job search, I'm trying to gather as much information and advice as possible before actually applying for a position. Could I take a few minutes of your time next week to discuss my career plans? I will call your office on Monday, Dec. 12, to see if such a meeting can be arranged.

I appreciate your consideration and look forward to meeting you.

Yours truly,


Hugh Beaumont

## After a job interview

1497 Lilac Street
Worcester, MA  01602
October 5, 2000

Mr. Rudy Delacort
Director of Personnel
Distinguished Fidelity
175 Boylston Avenue
Boston, MA  01949

Dear Mr. Delacort:

Thank you for the opportunity to interview yesterday for the analyst trainee position. I enjoyed meeting you and Cliff Stoudt, and learning more about Distinguished Fidelity.

Your organization appears to be growing in a direction that parallels my interests and career goals. The interview with you and your staff confirmed my initial positive impressions of Distinguished Fidelity, and I want to reiterate my strong interest in working for you. My prior experience as treasurer of my class, plus my Business College training in accounting and finance would enable me to progress steadily through your training program and become a productive member of your research team.

Again, thank you for your consideration. If you need any additional information from me, please feel free to call.

Yours truly,


Hugh Beaumont

## After an informational interview

Lazelle Wright
921 West Fourth Street
Steamboat Springs, CO  80477
303-555-3030
lazlo@mycomp.com

May 21, 2001

Mr. James R. Payne
Marketing Manager
Dutton & Dutton
241 Snowridge
Ogden, UT  84844

Dear Mr. Payne:

Jinny Clausewitz was right when she said you would be most helpful in advising me on a career in marketing.

I appreciate your taking the time from your busy schedule to meet with me. Your advice was most helpful, and I have incorporated your suggestions into my resume. I will send you a copy next week.

Again, thanks so much for your assistance. As you suggested, I will contact Joe Simmons at Datatek next week in regards to a possible opening with his company.

Sincerely,

Lazelle Wright

## Accepting a job offer

6227 Lochlevin Cove
Paramus, NJ 07652
October 5, 2001

Mr. Rudy Delacort
Director of Personnel
Distinguished Fidelity
175 Boylston Avenue
Boston, MA 01949

Dear Mr. Delacort:

I want to thank you and Mr. Stoudt for giving me the opportunity to work for Distinguished Fidelity. I am very pleased to accept the position as an analyst trainee with your Investment Unit. The position entails exactly the kind of work I want to do, and I know that I will do a good job for you.

As we discussed, I shall begin work on Dec. 1, 2001. In the interim, I shall complete all the necessary employment forms, obtain the required physical examination, and locate housing. I plan to be in Boston within the next two weeks and would like to deliver the paperwork to you personally. At that time, we could handle any remaining items pertaining to my employment. I'll call next week to schedule an appointment with you.

Sincerely yours,


Edward J. Haskell

cc:  Mr. Cliff Stoudt
      Investment Unit

## In response to rejection

709 Bernardi Street
Syracuse, NY 13210
October 5, 2001

Mr. Rudy Delacort
Director of Personnel
Distinguished Fidelity
175 Boylston Avenue
Boston, MA 01949

Dear Mr. Delacort:

Thank you for giving me the opportunity to interview for the analyst trainee position. I appreciate your consideration and interest in me.

Although I am disappointed in not being selected for your current vacancy, I want you to know that I appreciate the courtesy and professionalism shown to me during the entire selection process. I enjoyed meeting you, Cliff Stoudt, and the other members of your research staff. My meetings confirmed that Distinguished Fidelity would be an exciting place to work and build a career.

I want to reiterate my strong interest in working for you. Please keep me in mind if a similar position becomes available in the near future.

Again, thank you for the opportunity to interview and best wishes to you and your staff.

Sincerely yours,


Anthony Dow

cc: Mr. Cliff Stoudt
　　 Investment Unit

## Withdrawing from consideration

33 Brown Circle
Memphis, TN 38119
October 5, 1995

Mr. Rudy Delacort, Director of Personnel
Distinguished Fidelity
175 Boylston Avenue
Boston, MA 01949

Dear Mr. Delacort:

It was indeed a pleasure meeting with you and Mr. Stoudt last week to discuss your needs for an analyst trainee.

As I discussed with you during our meetings, I believe one purpose of preliminary interviews is to explore areas of mutual interest and to assess the fit between the individual and the position. After careful consideration, I have decided to withdraw from consideration for the position.

My decision is based upon two factors. First, the emphasis on data entry is certainly needed in your case, but I would prefer more balance in my work activities. Second, the position would require more travel than I am willing to accept with my other responsibilities.

I want to thank you for interviewing me and giving me the opportunity to learn about your needs. You have a fine staff and I would have enjoyed working with them.

Yours truly,


Barbara Billingsly


cc: Mr. Cliff Stoudt
    Investment Unit

# Chapter 12

# No More Sweaty Palms

You did weeks of research, constructed a professional-looking resume, contacted anyone you ever knew, and wrote brilliant cover letters to the handful of companies that you hoped were perfect for you. Unfortunately, all of this hard work will turn out to be meaningless if you're unable to convince one of those firms to actually hire you!

Look at the positive: If you were able to set up an interview at any of these companies, your resume and cover letter obviously peaked *someone's* interest. So there's only one minefield left to traverse—the job interview itself. It's time to make all that hard work pay off.

I'm not going to sugarcoat things. The fact is, job interviews have gotten a lot tougher. They tend to be more stressful—often requiring you to confidently declare how you might handle a number of "typical" scenarios. And it probably won't cheer you to know that the whole process is longer, too. These days you may be interviewed by half a dozen people before an offer is tendered.

Nervous?

Don't be. This chapter will put the interview process in perspective, giving you the "inside story" on what to expect and how to handle the questions and circumstances that arise during the course of a normal interview.

## This will hurt only a little bit

Interviews shouldn't scare you if you think of them as your chance to experience a company firsthand—"up close and personal."

The interviewer's questions will have but one purpose—to see if you are right for the company. Once you are in the interview "hot seat," your job is to convince the interviewer that you are the absolutely best candidate, that you will fit in and that you will be an asset to the company now and in the future. But while all of this is going on, you should also be thinking about one more thing—whether the company is right for *you*.

I hope this chapter convinces you to approach the interview with a little enthusiasm, calm yourself before sitting down in front of the interviewer, and let your personality do the work.

# It takes more than an ounce of preparation

By now you know that there is nothing like preparation to ensure success. This chapter will focus on the kinds of questions you are likely to be asked and guide you in answering them. It will also prompt you to develop your own list of questions to ask the interviewer.

The research you did to find the right industry is nothing compared to the research you must do now that you're narrowing your search to specific companies. Here's a complete checklist of the facts you should know about each company at which you schedule an interview:

## The basics

1. Directions to the office you're visiting.
2. Headquarters location (if different).
3. Some idea of domestic and international branches.
4. Relative size (compared to other companies in the field).
5. Annual billings, sales, and/or income (last two years).
6. Subsidiary companies; specialized divisions.
7. Departments (overall structure).
8. Major accounts, products, or services.
9. Major competitors.

## The subtleties

1. History of the firm (specialties, honors, awards, famous names).
2. Names, titles, and backgrounds of top management.
3. Existence (and type) of training program.
4. Relocation policy.
5. Relative salaries (compared to other companies in field or by size).
6. Recent developments concerning the company and its products or services (from your trade magazine and newspaper reading).
7. Everything you can learn about the career, likes, and dislikes of the person(s) interviewing you.

The amount of time and work necessary to be this well-prepared for an interview is considerable. You might find that some information you need is not readily available. (To find out how you can get this information, refer back to Chapter 2.)

Learning about your interviewer, on the other hand, is usually even more of a chore. But keep in mind that your investigation might give you the one nugget of information that will tip the scales and land you the job. Start with the biographical references listed in Chapter 2. If your interviewer is listed in any of these sources, you'll be able to learn a lot about his or her background. In addition, find out if he or she has written any articles or been interviewed in the trade press. Referring to these articles (assuming, of course, that they are favorable) can also set you apart from other candidates during the interview. You might also check to see if any of your networking contacts has ever worked with your prospective interviewer. One or more of them may be able to help fill in gaps in your information.

Suffice it to say that all of this new research will not be accomplished the day before the interview!

Is it really so important to go through all of this? Well, you can bet that *somebody* out there will spend the time and effort to become more knowledgeable before the interview. Can you guarantee that that somebody won't be competing for the job *you* want? If you don't take the time to prepare, which of the two of you do you think will impress the interviewer more?

## Surviving the "screen"

The majority of this chapter is devoted to the actual selection interview, which is usually conducted by the person to whom you will be reporting. But there is another process—the screening interview—which many of you may have to survive first.

At large companies, screening interviews are usually conducted by members of the Human Resources or Personnel department. Though they may not be empowered to hire, they are in a position to screen out or eliminate those candidates they feel are not qualified to handle the job. These decisions are not usually made on the basis of personality, appearance, eloquence, persuasiveness, or any other subjective criteria. Rather, they are made by clicking off "yes" or "no" answers against a checklist of skills. If you don't have the requisite abilities and track record, you will be eliminated from further consideration. With the rise of electronic submissions, the screener may be the computer program that looks for "key words" on the resume. If they're missing from yours, you just missed out on an interview.

This may seem cold, but it is a realistic and often necessary way for corporations to minimize the time and dollars involved in filling all top executive positions, and especially *entry*-level jobs.

These screening personnel are not looking for reasons to hire you—they're trying to find ways to eliminate you from the job search pack. Resumes sent blindly to Human Resources will usually be subjected to such impersonal screening. You probably will be eliminated without any real human contact (an excellent reason to construct a superior resume and not send out blind mailings).

At smaller companies, the founder, CEO, or another high-level executive may do his or her own screening. Their purpose is the same—to talk to many potential candidates in the least amount of time—but they differ from the other screeners in one important respect: They clearly have the power to hire. So make sure you know to whom you are talking.

If you are contacted for such an initial interview, it will most likely be by telephone. When you respond to a call from a prospective employer, keep these three things in mind:

1. This, too, is an interview. So be on your guard.
2. Answer all questions honestly.
3. Be enthusiastic.

You can expect the standard questions from the interviewer, who is attempting to "flesh out" the information included on your resume and/ or cover letter. If your resume is factual (and it should be), you have no reason to be anxious.

Don't be nervous—be glad you were called. And remember your objective: to get past this screening phase so you can get on to the real interview.

## The day of the interview

On the day of the interview, wear a conservative (not funereal) business suit—not a sports coat, not a "nice" blouse and skirt, nothing low-cut or tight-fitting. Your shoes should be shined, your nails cleaned, and your hair neatly styled.

It's not unusual for resumes and cover letters to head in different directions when a company starts passing them around to a number of executives. By the time of your interview, yours may be long gone, so bring along extra copies of your resume and your own copy of the cover letter that originally accompanied it. If appropriate or required, make sure you bring samples of your work (e.g., clippings, your portfolio, etc.).

### One, two, three...red light!

There are actions and answers that are guaranteed to make virtually any interviewer cringe and tempt him to simply suggest you try another company. I'm going to discuss some of them later in the chapter, but here is a full list of don'ts:

- Poor grooming
- Showing up late
- Inappropriate dress
- Any answer, no matter how detailed, that simply does not answer the question asked
- Defensiveness, especially if it's about something that doesn't appear to need defending
- Lack of knowledge of the company, job or industry, indicating poor or nonexistent research and preparation
- Dishonesty
- Lack of enthusiasm/interest
- Asking the wrong questions (e.g., about vacations, sick days, etc.)
- Any answer that clearly demonstrates you are unqualified for the job

+ Any disparity between your resume and interview answers (such as providing details on jobs not on your resume)
+ Lack of focus
+ Lack of eye contact
+ Any negativity, especially discussing people (your last boss, co-workers, etc.)
+ Inability to take responsibility for failures/weaknesses/bad decisions/bad results
+ Taking full credit for what was clearly a success to which others contributed

While most interviewers won't consider one of these an automatic reason to curtail the interview (with the notable exception of dishonesty), accumulating two or more may force even the friendliest to question your suitability

## "On time" means 15 minutes early

Plan to arrive 15 minutes before your scheduled appointment. If you're in an unfamiliar city or have a long drive, allow extra time for the unexpected delays that seem to occur with mind-numbing regularity on important days.

Arriving early will give you time to check your appearance, catch your breath, check in with the receptionist, learn how to pronounce the interviewer's name correctly—in other words, to get organized and battle-ready.

If you're late, you have at least one strike against you (with some interviewers, you will have already struck out), so *don't be late*. If you are unavoidably detained more than 10 minutes, call and offer to reschedule (after giving a truthful explanation of how you could possibly have allowed yourself to be late). Don't be surprised if some interviewers do not accept your offer. Nobody said it was fair out there.

### The eyes have it

When you meet the interviewer, shake hands firmly. People notice handshakes and often form a first impression based solely on them.

Try to maintain eye contact—continually but not constantly—with the interviewer as you talk. This will indicate you're interested in what he or she has to say. Sit straight with your hands folded and, of course, don't smoke.

Be careful about the "innocent questions" that almost invariably occur at the beginning of interviews—"How are you today?" or "Did you have any trouble finding us?" Even if you feel terrible that day and got lost because the interviewer gave you lousy directions, say that you're fine and you had no problem finding the place. Enthusiasm—about almost everything—is a plus.

Should coffee or a soft drink be offered, you may accept, but only if the interviewer is joining you).

Keep your voice at a comfortable level. Again, try to sound enthusiastic (without imitating Charlene Cheerleader). Just be yourself. Try to act like you're comfortable and enjoying the process. If you focus on remaining confident and poised, you should be able to provide direct, accurate, and honest answers to even the trickiest questions.

### Don't name-drop conspicuously

A friendly relationship with other company employees might have provided you with valuable information prior to the interview, but don't flaunt or dwell on these relationships. The interviewer is interested only in how *you* will relate to him or her and how well you might fit in with the rest of the staff. Name-dropping may smack of favoritism. And you are in no position to know who the interviewer's favorite (or least favorite) people are.

### Fork on the left, knife on the right

Interviews are sometimes conducted over lunch, although this is not usually the case with entry-level people. If it does happen to you, however, try to order something in the middle price range, neither filet mignon nor a cheeseburger. For many people, pasta can be a challenge. And spinach and a few other foods have a way of wedging between your teeth.

Do not order alcohol. If your interviewer orders a carafe of wine, you may share it, *sparingly*. Otherwise, alcohol should be considered *verboten* under all circumstances. Then hope your mother taught you the correct way to eat and talk at the same time. If not, just do your best to maintain your poise.

### The importance of last impressions

There are some things interviewers will always view with displeasure: street language, a complete lack of eye contact, insufficient or vague explanations or answers, a noticeable lack of energy, poor interpersonal skills (i.e., not listening or the basic inability to carry on an intelligent conversation), and a demonstrable lack of motivation.

Even *last* impressions count. So, before you allow an interview to end, summarize why you want the job, why you are qualified, and what, in particular, you can offer the company.

Then, take some action. If the interviewer hasn't told you about the rest of the interview process and/or where you stand, ask him or her: "What's the next step?" or "When can I expect to hear from you about a second interview?"

When you return home, file all the business cards, copies of correspondence, and notes from the interview(s) with each company in the appropriate files. Finally, but most importantly, ask yourself which firms you really want to work for and which you are no longer interested in. This will quickly determine how far you want the process to develop at each company before you politely tell them to stop considering you for the job.

Immediately send a thank-you letter to each executive you met. If you are still interested in pursuing a position at the company, communicate that in no uncertain terms. Reiterate why you feel you're the best candidate, and tell each of the executives that you hope to hear from them soon.

## On the eighth day, God created interviewers

Although most interviews will follow a relatively standard format, there will undoubtedly be a wide disparity in the skills of the interviewers you meet. Many of these executives (with the exception of the Human Resources staff) don't have extensive interviewing experience, have limited knowledge of interviewing techniques, are harried by the press of other duties, or simply don't view your interview as critically important.

Rather than studying standardized test results or utilizing professional evaluation skills, these non-professionals react intuitively—their initial (first five minutes) impressions are often lasting—even overriding other more important factors. So you must sell yourself...*fast*.

The best way to do this is to work at achieving a comfort level with your interviewer, just as you would in any social situation. Establish a rapport through words, gestures, common interests, etc.

## The set sequence

You can anticipate an interview sequence roughly as follows:
+ Greetings.
+ Social niceties (small talk).
+ Purpose of meeting. ("Let's get down to business.")
+ Broad questions/answers.
+ Specific questions/answers.
+ In-depth discussion of company, job, and opportunity.
+ Summarizing information given and received.
+ Possible salary probe (dependent upon level of achievement).
+ Summary/indication as to next steps.

## It's time to play Q & A

Many of the same questions pop up in interview after interview, regardless of company size, type, or location. I have chosen the 13 most common—along with appropriate hints and answers for each—for inclusion in this chapter. (If you want to prepare for 88 more, I suggest a copy of my *101 Great Answers to the Toughest Interview Questions*.) Remember: There are no right or wrong answers to these questions, only strong and weak ones.

Substance counts more than speed when answering questions. Take your time, and make sure that you listen to each question. There is nothing quite as disquieting as a lengthy, well-thought-out answer that is completely irrelevant to the question asked. You wind up looking like a programmed clone with stock answers to dozens of questions who has, unfortunately, pulled the wrong one out of the grab bag. (For an example of this, just watch a press conference on C-Span sometime!)

Once you have adequately answered a specific question, it is okay to go beyond it and add more information if doing so adds something to the discussion and/or highlights a particular strength, skill, course, etc. But avoid making lengthy speeches just for the sake of sounding off.

My advice is to study the list of questions (and hints) that follow, and prepare at least one solid, concise answer for each. Practice with a friend until your answers to these most-asked questions sound intelligent, professional, and, most importantly, spontaneous and unrehearsed.

### "Why do you want to be in this field?"

Using your knowledge and understanding of the particular field, explain why you find the business exciting and how you see yourself fitting in. If the job for which you're interviewing bears little or no relation to your major, be prepared to explain how the skills required in your degree field transfer to the field in which you're seeking employment. It is not *that* unusual to go into a field other than your major, but the more jarring the disparity (interviewing at a children's publishing company when your major was geology), the more prepared you should be to explain it.

### "So, tell me a little about yourself."

This question trips up many a candidate. It seems so easy, but only the most obnoxious people can talk about themselves at length without becoming self-conscious.

Using the information from your self-evaluation and the research you did on that particular company, formulate an answer that marries your strengths to their needs and to the characteristics of the position for which you're applying. Your answer should be no more than 250 words long— about one typewritten, double-spaced page. It should sound conversational, even though you'll have it memorized *cold*.

Summarize your resume—briefly—and expand on particular courses or experiences relevant to the firm or position for which you're interviewing. Do not go on about your hobbies or personal life, where you spent your summer vacation, or anything that is not relevant to securing that particular job. You may explain how the job fits in with your long-range career goals and talk about what attracted you to the company in the first place.

There are many variations on this question: What makes you special? What five adjectives describe you best? Rate yourself on a scale of 1 to 10. How would you describe your character? A more aggressive interviewer might ask: Why should I consider you a strong candidate for this position? What's better about you than the others candidates I've interviewed? What can you do for us that someone else can't?

Despite their differences, every one of these questions is trying to unearth *exactly* the same information: What *can* you do? What have you *done?* Are those the skills and experience the job requires?

### "Why did you choose our company?"

This question provides you with an excellent opportunity to explain the extensive process of education and research you've undertaken. Tell the interviewer about your strengths and how they match up with the job. Emphasize specific things about the company that led you to seek an interview. Be convincing. Bad answer: "So I'll have the shortest possible commute."

### "What can you do for us?"

Construct an answer that essentially lists your strengths, the experience you have that will contribute to your job performance and any other unique qualifications that will place you at the head of the applicant pack. Be careful: This is a question specifically designed to eliminate some of that pack. Sell yourself. Be one of the few called back for a second interview.

### "What position here interests you?"

If you're interviewing for a specific position, answer accordingly. If you want to make sure you don't close the door on other opportunities of which you might be unaware, you can follow up with your own question: "I'm here to apply for your Account Executive Training Program. Is there another position open for which you feel I'm qualified?"

If you've arranged an interview with a company without knowing of any specific openings, use the answer to this question to describe the kind of work you'd like to do and why you're qualified to do it. Avoid mentioning a specific job title, because titles tend to vary from firm to firm.

If you're on a first interview with Human Resources, just answer the question. They only want to figure out where to send you next.

### "What jobs have you held and why did you leave them?"

Or what they're *really* wondering: "Have you ever been fired?" Take this opportunity to expand on your resume, rather than precisely answering the question. In discussing each job, point out what you liked about it, what factors led to your leaving, and how the next job added to your continuing professional education. Don't be tempted to transform a summer stocking grocery shelves into a "better sounding" position, but do find a way to connect whatever skills you developed, no matter how minor, with the job you're seeking.

If you *have* been fired, say so. It's very easy to check. Try to avoid being defensive or blaming your fate on everyone else but yourself.

*"What are your strengths and weaknesses?"*

Be careful of being too forthcoming about your glaring faults (nobody expects you to volunteer every weakness and mistake). But do not reply, "I don't have any." They won't believe you and, what's worse, *you* won't believe you. After all, you did the evaluation—you know it's not true!

Good answers to these questions are those in which the interviewer can identify benefits for himself or herself and his or her department or company. For example: "I consider myself an excellent planner. I am seldom caught by surprise, and I pride myself on being able to anticipate problems and schedule my time to be ahead of the game. I devote a prescribed number of hours each week to this activity. I've noticed that many people just react. If you plan ahead, you should be able to cut off most problems before they arise."

You may consider disarming the interviewer by admitting a weakness, but doing it in such a way as to make it relatively unimportant to the job function. For example: "Higher mathematics has never been my strong suit. Though I am competent enough, I've always envied my friends with more mathematical ability. In sales, though, I'm certainly quick enough to figure out how large an order to ask for."

## *"Do you think your extracurricular activities were worth the time you devoted to them?"*

This is a question often asked of entry-level candidates. One possible answer: "Very definitely. As you see from my resume, I have been quite active in the Student Government and French club. My language fluency allowed me to spend my junior year abroad as an exchange student, and working in a functioning government gave me firsthand knowledge of what can be accomplished in the real world. I suspect my marks would have been somewhat higher had I not taken on so many activities outside of school, but I feel the balance they gave me contributed significantly to my overall growth as a person."

*"What are your career goals?"*

Interviewers are always seeking to probe the motivations of prospective employees. Nowhere is this more apparent than when the area of ambition is discussed. The high-key answer to this question might be; "Given hard work, company growth, and a few lucky breaks along the way, I'd look forward to being in a top executive position by the time I'm 35. I believe in effort and the risk/reward system—my research on this company has shown me that it operates on the same principles. I would hope it would select its future leaders from those people who display such characteristics."

### *"At some future date would you be willing to relocate?"*

Pulling up one's roots is not the easiest thing in the world to do, but it is often a fact of life in the corporate world. If you're serious about your career (and such a move often represents a step up the career ladder), you will probably not mind moving on...someday. If you really don't want to move, you may want to say so, too—though I would find out how probable or frequent such relocations would be before closing the door while you're still at the interview stage.

Keep in mind that as you get older, establish ties in a particular community, marry, have children, etc., you will inevitably feel less jubilation at the thought of moving once a year or even "being out on the road." So take the opportunity to experience new places and activities while you're young.

### *"How did you get along with your last supervisor?"*

This question is designed to understand your relationship with (and reaction to) authority. Remember: Companies look for team players, people who will fit in with their ways of doing things. An answer might be: "I prefer to work with bright, ambitious people who know what they want and can express themselves. I learned in the military that in order to accomplish the mission, someone has to be the leader and that person has to be given the authority to lead. Someday I aim to be that leader. I hope, then, that my subordinates will follow me as much and as competently as I'm ready to follow now."

### *"What are your salary requirements?"*

If they are at all interested in you, this question will probably come up. But every expert I've interviewed said emphatically that job-seekers should wait until they receive a firm offer before discussing compensation. Should the company decide you're their top candidate, you'll be in a much stronger negotiating position than if you reveal your salary requirements up front.

If the interviewer asks you during your first meeting how much money you expect, don't refuse to answer the question, but avoid being specific. Try this response:

"I'd like to know a little more about the job responsibilities and the level of expertise you're expecting before we discuss salary."

If pressed, you should still avoid committing yourself to a specific salary requirement. Instead, offer a broad range, saying something like:

"I expect that a company such as this would pay a fair market wage for the position, which I believe is in the $22,000 to $28,000 range."

Always give a fairly broad range. The bottom figure should be the minimum *you* will accept—not the minimum salary paid in your field.

# The not-so-obvious questions

All interviewers are different and, unfortunately, no rules stipulate that they must use all or any of the "basic" questions covered above. Most interviewers like to come up with questions that are "uniquely theirs," questions that seem to come out of left field. If asked, "What is your favorite ice-cream flavor?" or, "How many Beatles albums do you own?" just stay relaxed and take a few seconds to frame a reasonably intelligent reply.

Some questions may be downright inappropriate. Young women, for example, may be asked about their plans for marriage and children. Don't call the interviewer a chauvinist (or worse). And don't point out that the question may be a little outside the law (it is, *very* much so). The non-professional interviewer may not realize such questions are illegal, and a huffy response might confuse, even anger, him or her.

Whenever any questions are raised about your personal life, it is much more effective to respond that you are very interested in the position and have no reason to believe that your personal life will preclude you from doing an excellent job.

## *"Do you have any questions?"*

This is often the last (and potentially fatal) question an interviewer will throw at you after an hour or two of grilling. Unless the interview has been very long and unusually thorough, you *should* have questions—about the job, the company, even the industry.

In preparing for the interview, develop a set of questions—at least five or six—to ask the interviewer. After all, while the interviewer is trying to find the right person for the job, *you* are trying to find the right job. So, you should be just as curious as he or she has been. Here's a short list of questions you may consider asking on any interview:

1. What will my typical day be like?
2. Why is this position open? May I speak with the person who held it previously?
3. Given my attitude and qualifications, how would you estimate my chances for career advancement at your company?
4. How would you characterize the management philosophy of your firm?
5. What characteristics do the successful _____ at your company have in common? (Fill in the blank with the appropriate title, such as "writers," "accountants," "salespeople," etc.)
6. What kind of training should I expect, and for how long?
7. Is a written job description available?
8. Where will I be working? May I see my office/cubicle/closet?
9. What hardware and software will I be using most?
10. Is relocation an option, a possibility, or a requirement?

Other questions about the company or position will be obvious—they're the areas your research hasn't been able to fill in. Ask the interviewer. But be careful and use common sense. No one is going to answer highly personal, rude or indiscreet questions. Even innocent questions can be misconstrued if you don't think about the best way to pose them before they fall trippingly off your tongue.

## A word about applications and tests

Though not part of the selection interview itself, job applications and psychological testing are often part of the pre-interview process. You should know something about them.

The job application is essentially a record-keeping exercise—simply the transfer of work experience and educational data from your resume to a printed application form. There is one difference however: Applications often require you to list references and salary levels you've achieved. Be sure to bring your list of references with you to any interview (so you can transfer the pertinent information), and don't lie about your salary history. This information is easy to check.

Many companies now use a variety of psychological tests as additional mechanisms to screen out "undesirable" candidates. Although the accuracy of these tests is subject to question, the companies that use them obviously believe they are effective for identifying applicants whose personalities would preclude their participating positively in a given work situation, especially those at the extreme ends of the behavior spectrum. The usefulness of these tests in predicting job accomplishment is considered limited, however. If you are normal (like most of the rest of us), you'll have no trouble with these tests and may even find them amusing. Just don't try to outsmart them—you could just wind up outsmarting yourself.

## One step closer to your goal

Your interview is over. Breathe a sigh of relief. Make your notes—you'll want to keep a file on the important things for use in your *next* interview. That's right. If this is your first interview, it is not likely to be your last. Some people consider one in 10 (one job offer for every 10 interviews) a good ratio. But don't get caught up in keeping score. If you are persistent, sooner or later you'll be hired. For the *right* job.

# Chapter 13

# For Women (Mostly)

Every generation of American women has been able to say, "Our mothers never had it so good."

Nevertheless, in many fields and positions, women still struggle to get equal pay for equal work, and many women striving to get ahead in the corporate world still hit their heads on the "glass ceiling."

More specifically—and to the heart of this chapter—women are more likely to face some rather difficult job-hunting scenarios. For instance, if a married couple is blessed with a child, they may decide one parent is going to stay home with the baby—yet 9,999 times out of 10,000, it's the *woman* who will put her career on hold and reenter the work force far in the future.

While most men start working as soon as they graduate and continue until they retire or hit the lottery, some women might do their first job search late in life. After years of being full-time homemakers, they might find themselves searching for work because they need to make ends meet, as a result of divorce, the death of a spouse, or just because they can't stand being cook/maid/driver.

## The glass ceiling and a few other obstacles

Despite the fact that women now comprise a large segment of the work force, they still have the deck stacked against them.

Male managers still tend to hire "in their own likeness," so while women total almost half the labor force, less than 10 percent occupy top executive-level jobs. More than a third of Fortune 1000 corporate boards still don't have even one woman director.

While most families need two incomes to survive these days, the average woman still earns approximately 70 cents for every dollar earned by a man. In some fields, women are not wanted at any level. Certain professions, such as nursing, teaching, and human resources, are still "female ghettoes," while better paying areas—construction, accounting, and engineering—are dominated by men.

## Under scrutiny

Women's resumes may be scrutinized more closely than men's for clues about age, marital, and family status.

Gaps in employment history on women's resumes are red flags to many hiring managers—they signal the presence of "young 'uns." And that implies to many employers that this applicant will need time off when the kids are sick, will be in a hurry to get home, and may often show up late. In the best of all possible worlds, they'd be worried about the same things occurring when their male employees became fathers. They don't.

Even women who spend a relatively short time away from the work force can find themselves on a "Mommy Track." In any kind of tight job market, many women quickly discover that the only way to gain both flexibility and career satisfaction is to become self-employed.

Even tougher struggles confront women who've never worked outside the home. They have no job histories, no idea of what the world of business is like and, worst of all, no experience in selling themselves.

And let's not forget the thousands of women who pull up their roots each year when their husbands are transferred to other cities.

Get the point? Sure, women have it better than their mothers ever did, but there's still a long way to go.

The rest of this chapter will provide advice on constructing a resume that will help solve at least some of these problems. You'll find more in-depth advice in *The Smart Woman's Guide to Resumes and Job Hunting* and *The Smart Woman's Guide to Interviewing and Salary Negotiation* (both from Career Press).

## Don't reveal what you don't want them to know

I've worked in publishing for almost my entire career. It's a line of work that often demands long hours. Unpleasant surprises from printers, authors, the art department, etc., may mean I have to work late or right through a weekend on a moment's notice. In the minds of many employers, this kind of schedule doesn't exactly mesh with the idea of motherhood. Yet, I've seen countless women include the number of children they have on the "Personal Data" sections of their resumes!

It is against the law for employers to ask applicants about marital or family status. They can ask such things as, "Are you able to work long hours occasionally?" If your answer is yes, you shouldn't risk casting a doubt in the employer's mind by volunteering information he is not allowed to ask for.

As a matter of fact, it's also ill-advised to tell employers that you're married. Many assume that childless married women will all become mothers sooner rather than later (or never) and, therefore, require maternity leave.

Sometimes it's a cold world out there. Accept that, and plan your job-hunting armed with that knowledge.

## Not all experience is paid

As a savvy job hunter, you should consider *all* of your experience when you write your resume, not just the jobs for which they were paid. Volunteer work can certainly say a lot about your character, organizational ability, leadership skills, and dedication—all traits employers are trying to measure during resume reviews and in-person interviews.

Let's take a closer look at Kimberly Schand, whose resume we included on page 140.

Kim had gotten her career off to a healthy start before devoting herself to her children more than eight years ago. Like many stay-at-home mothers, Kim became involved in volunteer activities. However, *un*like most, she committed herself to these activities with the same drive that had characterized her early career.

She became a leader, directing activities and making decisions involving thousands of dollars. She committed countless hours to phone calls, meetings, planning, letter writing—in short, all of the headaches of a "real" job, but without a paycheck.

Now that her kids are in school, Kim is ready to get back to professional (i.e., "paid") work. She wants to channel her experience and interests into publicity and promotion, and has learned of an opening for a promotions coordinator at a local corporation.

At first, she designed her resume as most people with her type of job history would: She put her paid experience and education first, then mentioned her volunteer accomplishments almost as an aside.

## The value of experience

Experience is experience. No one should feel that their volunteer experience is any less valuable than paid experience might have been. When Kim spoke to a career counselor, he advised her to put together a resume that showed stability, reliability, and growth. Despite the fact that Kim didn't receive a paycheck for nearly a decade, she grouped all her experience together and presented it in chronological order, so that volunteer work received even more prominence than paid work.

The result is a clear and concise portrait of a woman who knows how to initiate, plan, organize, implement, and launch successful promotions.

## That's none of your business

The only other special advice I have for women has to do with recognizing and dealing with discriminatory statements and questions during job interviews (although certainly men can be subjected to some of these, too).

It's pretty easy to tell when a question is inappropriate—it has little or nothing to do with how you, as a prospective candidate, might perform on the job. And that's pretty much what the law states: Interviewers can ask questions that have to do with job performance only. When they ask questions that are unrelated to the work to be performed, they could be walking on thin ice. Here are some general guidelines that may help you recognize illegal or discriminatory questions:

**Name.** Sure, that seems innocent enough. Prospective employers will need to know your name to address you. But in many states, you are protected from questions that seek to determine your birth name if you've had it legally changed, or your maiden name if you're a married woman.

However, employees are permitted to ask what other names they should check to determine your employment history.

**Marital/family status.** Employers are not permitted to ask about your marital status or plans for marriage. Likewise, they are forbidden from asking women about their plans for having children.

I think this is an area in which it is very easy for you to "open the door" to a host of questions you aren't required to answer—unless *you* bring them up. After all, what could seem more innocent than chit-chatting about your fiancée, spouse, or kids? Do you really want to discuss your tentative plans for having a child within a year? Think about it.

**Age.** Employers cannot ask for your birth date or about facts that might reveal your birth date.

**Creed.** Under no circumstances is an employer permitted to ask about your religious affiliation or the religious holidays you observe. In addition, interviewers are not permitted to make even simple statements such as, "This is a Christian (or Jewish, or Muslim) company," perhaps looking for some sort of reaction from you as a prospective employee.

**Nationality.** Employers are generally forbidden to ask about your ancestry, descent, parentage, or nationality, that of your parents or spouse, or inquire about your "mother tongue."

**Race.** Employers cannot ask you about the color of your skin or that of your relatives or spouse.

**Military service.** The employer can ask how long and in what branch of the service you were in, but not the type of discharge you received.

**Physical condition.** Employers can ask if you have any physical conditions that might impede your performance on the job, but they cannot ask something like, "Do you have any physical disabilities?"

**Photographs.** Employers are not permitted to ask for photographs to be attached to job applications, unless the job, such as modeling or acting, requires it.

**Organizations.** Employers can ask about your membership in organizations that you consider important to the performance of the job. Otherwise, this can be another sneaky way to find out about religion (if you're a member of B'nai B'rith or the Christian Church Fellowship, for example), race (if you're a member of the NAACP and it's not obvious you are African American), political affiliation, etc.

Never bring up personal material yourself unless you're willing to answer questions about it. Savvy interviewers will grab at any opportunity to get information they want without running the risk of ending up in court. Their defense will be, "I never asked about her family. She brought it up."

If an interviewer is asking questions you feel shouldn't be asked, the first step is to shrug them off and deftly change the subject. The untrained interviewer may not realize he or she is doing anything inappropriate. Give him or her the benefit of the doubt. You may even warn—subtly—that you know your rights and don't wish to answer such questions. If the interviewer persists, consider ending the interview. Would you really want to work for a company or person that seems more interested in your heritage, skin color, or religion than your qualifications for the job?

What do you do with the prehistoric slob who uses the interview as an excuse to ask for a date? (Yes, it has and will continue to happen.) I'd end the interview as soon as possible and move on to the next company. That kind of situation is not likely to improve after you're on the job. While you may still want to investigate job possibilities in other departments or divisions, I'd think twice about a company that tolerates such behavior at all.

# Chapter 14

# Take That First Step

"The journey of a thousand miles begins with one step," was one of the many wise things Confucius said. Yet another was, "If you don't know where you're going, any road will take you there."

I know the prospect of drafting a resume, conducting a job search campaign, and going on interviews is daunting. How could it not be?

But the best way to conquer fear is knowledge. And the surest way to feel in control, rather than at the mercy of chance, is action.

I urge you—if you haven't already—to go through this book step by step. The successful job search is a process, one that demands that you decide what you want to do with your life, determine what it is you are most suited to do among those choices, and then find a company willing to pay you to do it.

I'm sure many of you purchased this book with the intention of "cutting to the chase" by adapting an already well-written resume to your purposes and getting it over with. Your resume should instead be thought of as a distillation of a great deal of reflection and work. In some ways, the resume is the road map that will help you decide where you are going in your career.

The only part of your resume that you should find easy to write is your name, address, phone numbers, and e-mail address. The career objective obviously should be the product of a great deal of thought. It will tell recruiters exactly what you are interested in, and help them determine quickly whether they should read on.

The rest of the resume must be thought of as a finely etched portrait of your achievements. It must convince a total stranger that he or she should trust you, live with you for about eight hours a day, and pay you.

Many people think of the resume as a formality. It is anything but. It must be a product of thought, time, and care if it is to help you get to where you want to go. Good luck in your job search. I hope this book helps you find a job that is well-suited to your talents and expectations.

# Take That First Step

# Index